I'm All In!

Lilia —

May this book inspire you to Rise to what your even higher Soul has already experienced.

Good Bless you

Keep Doing White

...

1-26-19

Front cover photo by Raquel P Photography
Back cover photo by Lourdes Velez
Cover design by Gia Rodriguez

Visit the author's website: www.AlonsoMinistries.org.

Library of Congress Control Number: 2017912036
International Standard Book Number: 978-1-62999-235-8
E-book International Standard Book Number: 978-1-62999-236-5

While the author has made every effort to provide accurate telephone numbers and Internet addresses at the time of publication, neither the publisher nor the author assumes any responsibility for errors or for changes that occur after publication.

First edition

17 18 19 20 21 — 987654321
Printed in the United States of America

Visit the author's website: www.AtanacioMinistries.com

Library of Congress Control Number: 2017908646
International Standard Book Number: 978-1-62999-235-8
e-book International Standard Book Number:
978-1-62999-236-5

While the author has made every effort to provide accurate telephone numbers and Internet addresses at the time of publication, neither the publisher nor the author assumes any responsibility for errors or for changes that occur after publication.

First edition

17 18 19 20 21 — 987654321
Printed in the United States of America

This book is primarily dedicated to my loving woman of faith, destiny partner, and supportive wife, Sandra Elizabeth Alonso, who has and continues to stand passionately by my side in the things of the kingdom. God blessed me with favor in having you as my ideal helpmate for my divine assignment. Thank You, God, and thank you, my love, for everything you do!

I also want to dedicate this book to my gentle warrior son, Andrew Michael Alonso, who is so connected with me in the Spirit. I love what you are becoming—a man unashamed of the gospel. I believe in you and all that God has in store for you.

Lastly, I want to dedicate this book to the amazing RiseUp Outreach faithful church members. You know who you are, as your fingerprints are all over this ministry! I cherish each of you and want you to know that your love and loyalty brighten my life. I wake up each day yearning to be the best I can be so that I can share the goodness God has poured into me with you. You are so very valued. You bring out the best in me, and I look forward to enjoying life together as I encourage you to RiseUp for His glory.

CONTENTS

CONTENTS

PREFACE

SOUTHWEST AIRLINES'S MOTTO boasts that when you fly their airline, "Bags Fly Free!" This may give you the idea that it's a necessity or even a luxury to carry extra baggage. However, where God is taking you, carrying extra baggage is unnecessary. Excess baggage will hinder, interfere, and delay your progress, purpose, and destiny. Anything that causes a dwindling in your joy, peace, or life must be laid aside so God can carry it. You don't need to go through life carrying all that junk in your trunk!

Sometimes it's not the big things that block our blessings, but the little things that we just can't seem to surrender. God wants us to *fully* yield so He can *fully* deliver us! As it is written, "Catch all the foxes, those little foxes, before they ruin the vineyard of love, for the grapevines are blossoming!" (Song of Sol. 2:15, NLT).

God is not a God of poverty; He is a God of prosperity. But don't be fooled into believing prosperity refers only to money—a false doctrine sorely overemphasized these days. God desires prosperity for your spirit, soul, body, and family, which will bring balance to your life. The ultimate gift you can give God is not your money, but *you*!

The person who chooses to remain in a safe, predictable, and secure setting rather than risk, surrender, and rise higher by faith in their God-given purpose will never reach the heights and fullness that our almighty God has set out for them. Following self-designed purpose rather than divine purpose brings displeasure to our Creator. God's reason for creating you was not for you to make money, get degrees, or even have a family. The reason God placed you on this earth and gave you a plan and a purpose was to qualify you to be an extension of heaven here on earth.

We only get one try at this thing called life. The main choice before us is whether we will live for our Lord Jesus Christ, who suffered, died, and was resurrected for us, or live for ourselves. I know it's challenging to deny ourselves, to pick up our cross daily and follow Jesus when this world's lures are so enticing. But the enemy doesn't show us the end product of that lure, though—for good reason. I also know there is a part of us that we want to hold back because of the uncertainty of what's ahead. However, God's promise to us when we surrender to Him and don't hold anything back is *life* for our eternal souls. I think that's worth the risk, don't you?

If you are always trying to be "normal," you will never know how amazing you can be! In 2 Chronicles 16:9 we read, "For the eyes of the LORD run to and fro throughout the whole earth, to show Himself strong on behalf of those whose heart is loyal to Him." Are you fully committed to God's way for your life, or is there still something inside of you that needs to be surrendered? I'm convinced the world has yet to see what God can do with and through the man who is *totally* committed to Him. If you are still hesitant, fearful, skeptical, or have contemplated living a life of full surrender but something always holds you back, this book is for you.

If you've been at the one-yard line for quite some time now, hesitating about crossing into the end zone and scoring that spiritual touchdown, then this book is for you. Living life with childlike faith, naked, unashamed, and surrendering *all* to your Creator in a life of abandon to Him will bring you greater results than playing it safe. What in the world is holding you back? What can this world give you that is better? How can the void and emptiness each soul carries be satisfied with anything better? A life surrendered to the One who loves you more than anyone is the best investment you can make for yourself, your family, and your future.

As you know, one day your life on this earth will come to an end. What will be said about your life? Did you live a life so focused on playing it safe, never taking a risk on what could have been, that you leave this world yearning and dissatisfied? You cannot discover the ocean unless you have the courage to lose sight of the shore. Where there's risk, there's always a reward—even if it's only learning a good lesson. I like what the late Jim Rohn said: "If you are not willing to risk the unusual, you will have to settle for the ordinary."[1]

God did not create us to be ordinary, nor does He want us to live safe, small lives wherein we keep to ourselves the precious spiritual gifts He gave to us. The Book of Acts in the New Testament is a story of ordinary men and women who did extraordinary things because they allowed God to have His way in their lives. In the same way, God wants to use you to turn your world upside down for Jesus. It starts with you coming to a point of surrender and saying, "Lord, I want to make a difference. Have Your way in me! Help me learn to surrender to Your perfect will, which will produce a much better harvest than mine. Rescue me from myself and my fears! I don't want this world to turn me around. I am sick and tired of being sick and tired! I'm tired of living an unfulfilled life because I'm serving two masters (You and me). I'm tired of living a powerless life. Use me according to Your plans and purposes so I can live whole, satisfied, and in Your fullness! I'm All In!"

ACKNOWLEDGMENTS

THERE ARE SO many people that have been positive influences in my life that I would need a separate chapter to name them all. Each nugget of wisdom shared has helped me become the man I am today. The Word teaches us to honor those who deserve to be honored, and this is one way I would like to recognize their support publicly. If you're one of these people and in reading this book find I didn't mention your name, I apologize and say a big "thank you!" I trust that your reward is not forgotten in heaven.

First of all, I want to thank my best friend, prayer partner, lover, destiny soul mate, woman of God, and precious wife, Sandra, for helping me to complete this book. She was so supportive and encouraging and kept reminding me that I needed to finish it. Thank you, my love, for your gentle pushes!

I want to thank my parents, Heriberto Alvaro Alonso and Loida Noemi Alonso, for raising me up in the ways of the Lord. Today I serve the King of kings as His chosen vessel because of your sacrifices, prayers, testimony, support, and love. Gracias.

I want to thank the late Reverend Jose "Pepito" Berrios for the powerful sermons of sweat, tears, and inspiration he would pour out to his congregation. He impacted me to embrace living in the fear of the Lord. I was always in awe, even as a nine-year-old boy, of God's anointing on his life. I miss him dearly, but one day we'll catch up in heaven.

I want to thank my brother, mentor, and friend, Apostle Lee Harris, who believed in me when I began my journey as a full-time minister, and who also ordained me for the heavenly assignment/calling that God placed on my life.

I want to thank my brother, mentor, and friend, Apostle Rufus Troup, who is a living testimony of faith, and who used his prophetic gift to declare a renewed spirit of boldness and courage for God over my life. Thank you for also being the minister who married my wife and me.

I want to humbly thank the RiseUp Outreach Center congregation, online viewers, radio listeners, and the Executive Committee Ministry Team for your generous support, loyalty, love, and commitment toward a spirit of excellence. You help my days be joyous!

I want to thank my editor, Maggie Schubert, for once again allowing God to use her gift for His kingdom's glory. You never asked for anything, expected nothing, and simply said, "I'll be glad to do it." You're a class act, and I know your reward in heaven is waiting.

Lastly, I want to thank EVERYBODY who had an impact in guiding me to the power of a made-up mind and an ALL IN surrendered heart for Jesus Christ, my Savior and Lord. My intention in writing this book is to pass on His blessings, help people RiseUp from their comfort zones, and to ultimately give God all the glory.

INTRODUCTION

IT'S TIME TO cross the one-yard line into the end zone and do away with the fear of the unknown, refusal to surrender control, indecisiveness, and the non-fulfilling safety of the comfort zone. It's time to RiseUp and be "ALL IN" for God so you can experience His fullness, inner freedom, peace, joy along with less stress and more stability.

Our choices and decisions will either point us to our history or point us to our divinely orchestrated destiny. The Bible mentions the drawbacks, penalties, and consequences of living in double-mindedness. Are you tired of your life being unstable? Do you constantly want to be in control rather than surrender to God's perfect will for your life? Do you fear how you will be perceived if you went "ALL IN" for God? How will your life change (for the better, may I add)? Are you having major challenges moving past a bad relationship? Are you getting frustrated in your teen parenting role? In summary, are you tired of being stuck in "progress land" when it comes to your life battles?

You've tried conquering your battles, challenges, and issues in your own strength, practiced yoga, tried higher education and nothing has provided the answer you seek. Well, rather than continue to punish yourself with this never ending stuck-cycle, learn the simple truth from this book - that life does not need to be lived in this way. It doesn't have to be so stressful. You don't have to live with such anxiety, lack of fulfillment, and instability. In this book, Heriberto "Hery" Alonso will emphasize:

- The power of a made-up mind-set in Christ Jesus (defeating double-mindedness).

- Benefits of living in the will of God rather than in our own.

- How to start your day right and finish strong (setting the tone).

- Trusting God when you can't trace His moves.

- Developing the fear of the Lord which is the beginning of wisdom.

- Ten ways to heal & let go of a tainted love and/or toxic romantic relationship.

- Twelve principles on how to improve your covenant marriage.

- Eight ways to become a better parent to your teenager.

- Moving pass stuck and recognizing life's passion killers.

- Why we need the fire of the Holy Spirit.

- How to be ALL IN for Jesus Christ (go from casual Christian fan to a true follower).

Everybody wants to live with peace, joy, and fulfillment, but not all are willing to make the necessary tough choices to achieve them. Changes in our lives don't just happen by osmosis. While the effort may be there, the lack of focus, fear, and inability to be ALL IN cause most to miss out on God's best. I pray this book will nullify past ways of thinking and impact you to an improved outlook. People have told me, "Pastor, you're so lucky." I usually respond, "No, I'm blessed and you have no idea how much I've prayed or the price I've paid."

Bottom line: life is a choice and those who continue to live passively rather than RiseUp for God will miss out on His best. I want to encourage you to be ALL IN and fight the good fight of faith. Good things don't come easy nor are they ours to keep without work. Adjustments, improvements, and tweaks need to be made as we examine ourselves.

My sincere hope with this book is that it impacts your life for the better by revealing the power of a true relationship with Jesus and that after reading it, you genuinely consider it a must read!

ways of thinking and impact you to an improved outlook. People have told me, "Pastor, you're so lucky." I usually respond, "No, I'm blessed and you have no idea how much I've prayed or the price I've paid."

bottom line: life is a choice and those who continue to live passively rather than blessfup for God will miss out on His best. I want to encourage you to be ALL IN and fight the good fight of faith. Good things don't come easy nor are they ours to keep without work. Adjustments, improvements, and tweaks need to be made as we examine ourselves.

My sincere hope with this book is that it impacts your life for the better by revealing the power of a true relationship with Jesus and that after reading it, you genuinely consider it a must read!

PART 1

SIMPLIFY YOUR LIFE

1

GOD'S WILL OR YOUR WILL?

Not everyone who says to Me, "Lord, Lord,"
shall enter the kingdom of heaven, but he
who does the will of My Father in heaven.
—MATTHEW 7:21

THE CLOSER A person walks to the perfect will of God, the more God reveals and upgrades His anointing in their life. However, many people are stalled at the one-yard line because they want to hold on to a part of themselves rather than cross over to God's unknown. They want to take 80 percent of the Bible and be their own free agent with the remaining 20 percent. I totally understand this mind-set, stet because I spent much of my early life believing that partial control was going to bring me the most satisfying results. My goodness, was I wrong!

Most of us (including me at one point in my life) miserably fail to surrender our will to almighty God. We know He wants all of us, but spiritual blindness continues to keep us in our perceived safe haven. The thrill of that touchdown celebration is waiting, but we don't like surprises. We don't like to be caught off guard. We want to be in control, or at the very least we want to call the shots in some situations. We're not quite ready to leave the things of this world that bring us a temporary rush and momentary pleasure. But rest assured that these things will later corrupt and entangle the soul, because they have been placed before us by the prince of darkness himself, who has created them as a trap for our dissatisfaction and destruction.

However, in order to be "all in" and embrace the fullness of joy, peace, and power in your life—not to mention allow your Creator to have His way in you, ultimately bringing the most fulfillment and satisfaction to your life—you will have to make a choice. And the choice to decide whose will you shall follow involves surrendering your own will as to who is Lord, who has priority, and whom you will serve.[1]

Ultimately, God's overall perfect will and plan shall manifest itself. But will His purpose, plans, and destiny for you do so? Only God knows, for His thoughts and ways are not ours. Sometimes you can say no in church and the next time you get a chance to say yes, you're in a hospital bed. Sooner or later, God will have His way! Whether you're rich or broke, God will have His way. Whether you're healthy or sick, God will have His way. Whether you're educated or illiterate, God will have His way. When you belong to God, God will have His way!

Many have come to me on this subject asking, "Pastor Hery, how do you know you're in the perfect will of God?" Usually they are just curious, but I think it's a great question. You know you are in the perfect will of God when you're growing and experiencing provision, favor, peace, and newfound relationships that are strategic in sustaining and preparing you for your purpose and journey.

However, when we no longer know the difference between what is holy and what is ungodly, we have lost sight of the will of God. The world's motto is "Do whatever you want, because it's your life." But God's plan is better than yours could ever be. Most people in the church today genuinely desire to rise up for God but continue to live in the past, continue to do their own will, and continue to live frustrated lives. Why? Because anything outside the perfect will of God brings unnecessary frustration. In order to rise up, you have to be ALL IN! You have the key to make the right decision, and the offering you can give to your Creator is your very own will.

God is working to better your life at this very moment. Just because you might not understand what is happening, this doesn't mean it is not part of His plan. As much as you want to plan your life, living in God's will leads to a life that has a way of surprising you with unexpected things that bring more fulfillment and joy than you could ever plan for yourself. That's what is called being in God's will.

However, do not be deceived like some people who think that when you're in the will of God, everything goes right. That is simply not true. You could be in the will of God and still get crucified. Jesus died for your salvation and your body; therefore, your body is not for you to do whatever you want with it. Do you love your life so much that you would be willing to be crucified for it at the cross? He loves you more than you love yourself; thus, it is His will that you should follow, and it is His voice only to which you should listen. Thank God that Jesus chose to do His Father's will, or else we would all be doomed to eternal damnation, separated from the Father for all time. This is why His name is above every other name and He gets the ultimate glory and the highest praise in the entire world.

Child of God, you need to get to that bold and courageous point when your will and God's will intercept by saying, "Lord, I want what You want!" May His will be done and yours be gone. May His will be exalted and yours be made obsolete. This, in a nutshell, is what being "ALL IN" means. Declaring or proclaiming this statement will take you to a place where you will have to forgive some people against whom you've been harboring resentment. It will cause you to disappoint some people. It will take you to the point of making tough decisions that don't necessarily leave you with clear answers. However, know that doing the will of God will bring the life of God to you. The life of God comes alive in you when you are doing the will of God, and with that comes many benefits. Allow me to share seven of them with you, along with applicable Bible verses, which I hope will encourage you to make that all-important jump.

BENEFITS OF DOING THE WILL OF GOD

1. IT KEEPS YOUR SPIRIT ALIVE AND KEEPS YOU THANKFUL

> Rejoice always, pray without ceasing, in everything give thanks; for this is the will of God in Christ Jesus for you. Do not quench the Spirit.
> —1 THESSALONIANS 5:16–19

God knows our future. For example, He knows that the person you currently think you cannot live without will become a distraction or even a destructive force in your life ten years from now. You need to trust God enough to thank Him when he does not answer your prayer!

2. SILENCE CAN'T FOOL US

> For this is the will of God, that by doing good you may put to silence the ignorance of foolish men.
> —1 PETER 2:15

Sometimes what we think is best in the natural is actually diametrically opposed to God's perfect will. His plans don't have to be reasonable or logical to us. But following His will is always the wisest way, and wisdom is always superior to even brilliant intelligence.

3. IT KEEPS YOU ON THE RIGHT PATH

> Trust in the Lord with all your heart, and lean not on your own understanding; in all your ways acknowledge Him, and He shall direct your paths.
> —PROVERBS 3:5–6

If there is a right time in the will of God, the wrong time is us jumping ahead. Stop living with an instant gratification mind-set! Just as the human gestation period for a pregnancy is nine months, unless there is a threat of life, we cannot rush to get that baby out in six or seven months.

Being in the will of God increases your faith and patience. It gives you the necessary endurance to trust in the inherited promises that He has for you. We may have the faith, but we also need the patience to trust in the set time that only God knows. Look what the Word of God says in Hebrews 6:12: "…that you do not become sluggish, but imitate those who through faith and patience inherit the promises."

When we hurry, we force things to happen that are not in accordance with His plans. Just because it's not happening doesn't mean the enemy is getting the best of you or that God has gone on vacation. One of the most costly decisions in the history of the world was when Sarah convinced Abraham to sleep with her maidservant, Hagar, to conceive the child God had promised them. However,

God had promised them a child from their own union. Foolishly they thought they could help God; they thought God had forgotten them. Hagar delivered a child who was named Ishmael, the father of the present-day Palestinians. Despite their disobedience, God was true to His promise and Sarah became pregnant and gave birth to Isaac, from whom the Jewish race descended. The Bible tells us that there will never be peace in the Middle East. That chaos continues there even today and will be present until the end times, all because of that rash decision.

I want to encourage you today to believe that if you trust in God's will, He will bring you His best, but in His set time. You don't need to force it, but you do need to let go of your Ishmael so that your Isaac can be on its way. Take the pressure off yourself and just surrender. You may think, "Well, Pastor Hery, what if it doesn't happen?" You must really believe that His perfect will for your best is coming. Suppose you were projected into the future to three years from today and God showed you how He answered your prayer. It would be easy to trust Him then, right? That trust is the kind you must have in the present—full belief that your set times are coming. It may not be in your timing, but it will be in God's precise timing. You can trust the faithfulness of God.

4. **MAKING DECISIONS BECOMES EASIER WHEN YOUR WILL TO PLEASE GOD BECOMES GREATER THAN YOUR WILL TO PLEASE THE WORLD.**

> Your ears shall hear a word behind you, saying,
> "This is the way, walk in it," whenever you turn to
> the right hand or whenever you turn to the left.
> —ISAIAH 30:21

Jesus went through temptations as you do, so you can surrender yourself fully to God. He will honor your tough decisions of obedience! Every day we are conflicted between the easy way versus the right way. The choices we make have everything to do with our end results. Therefore, be wise not to make permanent decisions in temporary situations.

5. It causes you to live mistake-free because the Spirit is never wrong

> Now He who searches the hearts knows what the mind of the Spirit is, because He makes intercession for the saints according to the will of God.
>
> —Romans 8:27

Many of us have short-changed and cheated ourselves because of our insistence on doing our own will. You believe that everybody is moving ahead of you while you are standing still. Ask God today to give you the grace to embrace the timing of His perfect will. You know you have made the right decision or can make the right decision when there is peace in your heart.

6. It brings God pleasure

> For it is God who works in you both to will and to do for His good pleasure.
>
> —Philippians 2:13

Many cannot surrender to God's perfect will and be ALL IN because they "feel" it is not the right way. Since when are fickle feelings so significant or trustworthy? Granted, they are somewhat important; however, I don't know about you, but most of my bad decisions have come about because I've followed my "gut" or "feelings" rather than what I knew was the will of God. As world-renowned author John Maxwell, wrote, "You must do right before you feel good."[2] Be more interested in pleasing God than in pleasing your feelings (and in pleasing other people, for that matter). We walk by faith, not by feelings. By what are you walking? Don't quit or walk away just because you've gotten your feelings hurt or because your feelings are not being satisfied. If you want heaven on earth, then do the will of God at whatever cost.

7. IT BRINGS YOU PEACE AND CALMNESS

> Be still, and know that I am God; I will be exalted
> among the nations, I will be exalted in the earth!
> —PSALM 46:10

In a crisis situation such as a job layoff, negative medical report, family issue, or any anxiety that deprives you of sleep, you best be sure that you turn to God's will. You really know who is and who is not in God's will when (not "if") a crisis comes into a person's life.

We don't have to worry about our future because God is already there. I love Psalm 31:15: "My times are in Your hand; deliver me from the hand of my enemies, and from those who persecute me." I am personally convinced that stress is the result of living outside the will of God. When a person is not ALL IN, he is walking in his own will, and that produces a gradual, internal death of the soul. Don't try to figure things out all the time or worry why things are not happening. Find rest in the everlasting arms of your heavenly Father. Sometimes God calms the storm, and sometimes He lets the storm rage and calms His child. Either way, you are going to win if you walk in His will and trust Him.

In conclusion, you will never know where God wants to take you until you are willing to leave where you are.

Just because salvation is free to receive, this doesn't mean that it won't cost you something to walk in the power and perfect will of God. Choose to DO the will of God so that the life of God will be in you, and when things don't go as planned, don't get discouraged. Be open to where God brings you and let Him use you how He really wants to. Sometimes what appears to be a setback ends up becoming a divine setup for God to position you in a place of favor and blessing! It may not seem like it right now, but God knows what He is doing in the midst of your chaos.

The beautiful thing about your plans falling apart is that you are then free to watch His plans unfold. However, we have to understand that there is a huge difference between God giving you something and you trying to force something that makes you constantly have to work and be burdened to keep it. You can do the *right* thing at the *wrong* time and miss out on God's best!

So often we foolishly think that we need to do things in our own strength or do things with Christ that are unacceptable in His eyes. Don't misinterpret the Scriptures to fit your own purpose or desires. You cannot do *all* things through Christ, only those things—despite how difficult or unlikely—that are in the will of God for your life through Christ. God is not going to strengthen you to do what He hasn't purposed for you. The grace and power of God is for doing the will of God.

The gospel is like a double-edged sword that cuts and transforms. It is part inspiration, but mainly revelation. At some point you have to grow; you cannot stay the same. The Word in fact instructs us to go from glory to glory (2 Cor. 3:18). If you are still in a warm and fuzzy stage after ten or fifteen years of being a Christian, I personally feel it's because you have chosen to do your will, not God's. His will is for you to grow to eat meat, not to stay hanging on to your milk bottle. This particular verse in Hebrews 6:1 backs me up: "Therefore, leaving the discussion of the elementary principles of Christ, let us go on to perfection, not laying again the foundation of repentance from dead works and of faith toward God." Keep in mind that emotions may be up and down, blessings will come and go, and feelings may be high or low, but as long as you're walking in the PERFECT will of God, you're good to go! Actually, the safest place in the entire world is the will of God! Stay there, live there, and close the blinds!

2

THE POWER OF CHOICES
AND DECISIONS

Then you will understand what it means to fear the
LORD, and you will gain knowledge of God. For
the LORD grants wisdom! From his mouth come
knowledge and understanding. He grants a treasure
of common sense to the honest. He is a shield to
those who walk with integrity. He guards the paths
of the just and protects those who are faithful to
him. Then you will understand what is right, just,
and fair, and you will find the right way to go.
—PROVERBS 2:5–9, NLT

SOMETIMES IN LIFE we try to do something over
which we have no control. However, for the most
part, life is a choice! Ah yes, the power of choice and
making a decision can radically change your life—for the
better or for the worse. "Choice" usually means choosing
something out of several options (cake, pie, sundae, etc.).
A decision is made regarding something you need to
solve. (Shall I leave him or stay and try to work it out?
Should I engage in that sin or should I resist?) We will
use them both as the same in this chapter since they are

synonymous. We all obviously have made wrong choices, but this book is tailored to give you a mental outline to make better decisions based on what is truly important and thus enjoy life to its fullest.

Let me begin by emphasizing that there is power in a made-up mind. I love this Bible verse in Colossians 3:2, which supports my belief: "Set your mind on things above, not on things on the earth." A person whose mind wavers is unstable in all his ways, but a person who makes up his mind and moves forward can turn his life around. What I believe this verse is also implying is that we need to make up our mind HERE before the temptation comes THERE. When a person is surprised by a temptation, it can be very challenging to do the right thing when his or her mind is not focused. You have to understand that your decisions decide the quality of your life. Many of us are headed down the wrong path without considering the consequences. Let me suggest that you pause for a moment and analyze your life. Why? Because if you do not change direction, you may end up where you are going!

I was able to turn my life around, and so can you—I have no doubt! It takes only a decision here and there, one at a time. It takes focus on what truly matters to set the right priorities of life. It takes a mind-set that stays on the right path with the almighty God. Making the right choices on the wrong path equates to struggling against the winds of life.

I simply decided to do things the right way and not my way. I was tired and frustrated from my plans not working out. I decided to turn it around because life seemed too overwhelming. Rather than me rising above the storms, the storms were beating me up. I would say almost within two to three years, my life turned around drastically and I felt better than I had in my previous forty-one years. I made bad decisions that got me in a hole, and I had to make good decisions to get myself out. It all didn't change right away, but I did see progress in some form or another with each passing day, and so will you.

When we wake up from our sleep, the mind throws many choices at us. Do I pray or not? Do I go to church or not? Do I read the Bible or not? Do I tithe or not? Do I work out or not? Do I goof off or not? Do I resist the enemy or do I let the flesh have its way? Do I do what I'm supposed to do with regard to family, friends, work, or school, or do whatever I feel like doing? Not doing anything is also making a choice. There are so many different directions to go, but all I know is that your life is supposed to mean something before you die. Your life is supposed to be fruitful, and if it's asking a lot from you, it's only because it knows there is a lot IN you.

The Bible warns us of the dangers and consequences of living lukewarm, ambivalent, or serving two masters. Ephesians 5:15–17 says, "See then that you walk circumspectly, not as fools but as wise, redeeming the time, because the days are evil. Therefore do not be unwise, but understand what the will of the Lord is." We all have sinned and probably will sin again in some form or fashion. However, continual and deliberate sinning causes calluses to form on the heart; almost like putting novocaine on the soul. The first time it could perhaps be a mistake, but the second time it's a choice. Sin gradually corrupts and causes part of our existence to die internally. Many people simply exist, not truly living, because they are not ALL IN for God. Keep going to church to grow in faith and getting close to the fire of God. Don't let your Saturday night affect your Sunday morning!

There are two things that determine who we become. One of them is our decisions. We have free will, the power to make our own choices, but our choices have the power to make us. Emotions play a key role in making wise decisions. Many times we make decisions because of pressure, status, what feels good (instead of what is right), or when we're hurried or angry. An important motto to memorize and employ the rest of your life is, "Wait to subside before you decide." In other words, make sure you cool off and don't make decisions while angry. Your decisions will be tested, and tests need to be passed. You pass tests by doing what is right. You can't go wrong doing what's right.

The other thing that determines who we become is our response to God. Do you have a rebellious or unteachable spirit? If you do, you probably do not take constructive criticism very well. I know I used to be like that, and I was doing myself a huge disservice. Let me assure you that your flesh is always telling you to hit the snooze button on things. Your flesh wants you to do things that are not pushing you toward your purpose. If you're not living on purpose, you will be driven by pressure, pleasure, popularity, power, prestige, possessions, your past, or your pains. The Spirit, on the other hand, is always pushing you, because we can't press in our flesh. Allow me to clarify. The Holy Spirit, which is our Counselor, is constantly sending signals to us to DO the will of God. This helps us to remain in right standing with Him. The flesh doesn't press; it just does whatever it feels like doing. You don't have to work at it, and it usually leans toward doing the opposite of God's will.

The Spirit of God leads us to make wise decisions that help us live a powerful life. The benefits—longevity, wealth, honor, a clear conscience, joy, and peace—that come when we make up our minds to listen to and obey the Spirit's calling are so worth it. Obeying the Spirit brings abundant fulfillment and satisfaction. You will be living in divine wisDOM rather than in worldly wisDUM.

When we apply divine wisdom to our choices and decisions, we stand out from the herd. This Bible verse will humble anybody who thinks they are all that with their limited intellect: "But God has chosen the foolish things of the world to put to shame the wise, and God has chosen the weak things of the world to put to shame the things which are mighty" (1 Cor. 1:27).

Allow me to share three powerful tips regarding decision making that will assist you when that moment arrives. The first one is to ask yourself, will this decision move me closer to my goal or my God? If yes, proceed. If no, stop and don't force it or try to run from it. The second tip is for you to make your decision quickly. Statistics indicate that your first choice in answering a question on an exam is usually the right answer. Many people erase their answer rather than sticking to the one that first came to their mind. Successful people make decisions quickly and change them slowly, if necessary. The last tip I want to leave you with is to live with your decision. Too many people start doubting their decisions right away. Don't— be bold! Double-mindedness is not just saying different things, but it's living in two different worlds.

If you don't know what to do regarding a difficult decision, then do what works, adding your common sense to the mix. I'm grateful for spiritual discernment, but I'm also grateful for common sense. The Bible says we are to walk in the Spirit. The Spirit is NEVER wrong and ALWAYS comes with peace. Unfortunately, most of us are either not mature enough in the faith or are not hungering or thirsting for righteousness to understand how it operates. Do you want to make the right decision every time? Let the Spirit lead. Keep putting yourself in a position of being constantly "filled" in the Spirit. Understand that when spiritual maturity stagnates, the Spirit of peace cannot guide us into making the right decision every time. When in doubt, do what the Word says, and the Word will tell your spirit man what to do.

When you face difficult decisions or uncertain choices, it also helps tremendously to seek counsel from someone you respect who is anchored in Christ. We should always be willing to take advice, as there is sound wisdom in counseling. Many times we become confused because we take our focus off of the One that brings peace. The Bible tells us in 1 Corinthians 14:33 that "God is not the author of confusion." So you know that if you are confused, it's not from God. We need to let peace be the umpire of our decisions, as it is written in Colossians 3:15, "And let the peace of God rule in your hearts." If you don't have peace, then keep it moving. Do not make any decision if there is any uneasiness in your soul.

START YOUR DAY RIGHT

One of the things I began to do that changed my life was to start my day with prayer. I began to command the mornings in prayer, which would anchor my soul soundly in God. By doing this regularly, I gradually set the tone and the mind-set for each day. I love what the psalmist wrote in Psalm 42:1: "As the deer pants for the water brooks, so pants my soul for You, O God." Furthermore, if Jesus, the Son of God, who was perfect, did it, how much more should we consider it? See for yourself in Mark 1:35: "Now in the morning, having risen a long while before daylight, He went out and departed to a solitary place; and there He prayed."

Something happens when we give God the first minutes or hour of our day (firstfruits), when the mind is fresh.

I can't explain it, but some of my most powerful prayers have come in the sunrise hour. An impactful shift occurs in the spirit of man that causes us to be focused, fearless, and powerful throughout the day. You have a better grip on life. You've just got to believe me and set your alarm clock to go off thirty minutes early to understand what I mean. I just put on some worship music and soak in His presence. Sometimes I pray by worshipping and praising Him or I will ask for help with my petitions; other times I just shut up and let His Spirit speak to mine.

Life is busy and filled with distractions. It's very easy to get caught up in our cares, errands, and concerns so that we lose sight of what truly matters most. The biggest hindrance to our choices or decision making is that our "feelings" get in the way. We make too many choices based on feelings without considering the consequences of those choices, especially choices that contaminate the soul because of the sin with which we've chosen to entangle ourselves.

If we don't take the time to pray for perseverance to press on, the waves of life will find a way to toss us to and fro. A prayerless Christian is pretty much a powerless Christian. In fact, if a person goes three months without praying, reading the Word, or going to church seeking God, it's pretty much over! They have drifted from what truly matters. They have lost their focus and the reason for their existence. Their faith can turn to doubt, and many will turn to worldly philosophy, cults, horoscopes, psychics, or witchcraft. This will bring unnecessary confusion, not to mention destroy any existing intimacy with God. We can never be too busy to pray, because prayer makes our lives much more focused, efficient, blessed, and peaceful. The late Martin Luther King Jr. said, "More work is done by prayer than by work itself."[1]

The greatest weapon we have against the attacks, snares, and traps of the enemy is prayer. Sometimes it's not about prayer, but simply commanding or speaking to the mountains of our lives in faith (as mentioned in Mark 11:23). Faith comes by hearing, and hearing, and hearing the Word of God. When there is abundance of faith in the heart, the mouth will know what to speak thereafter. Many don't know what to pray for or how to cast down a mountain (major problem or issue) because they are consumed by fear and lacking in faith. If your faith isn't strong enough to move your mouth, then it isn't strong enough to move your mountain.

Spiritual warfare is not fought with natural weapons. We are not fighting against flesh and blood throughout the day, but against principalities of darkness. If we were to see what's really going on in the spiritual world, we would be blown away. We would witness Satan and his demons here and there, and the Holy Spirit and His ministering angels fighting them on our behalf. But take heart—there is nothing to fear. The enemy may have power, but we have been given authority and dominion to cast out anything that comes against us, our families, or our circumstances. The Bible clearly tells us that no weapons formed against us shall prosper (Isa. 54:17), because greater is He that is in us than he that is in the world (1 John 4:4). Glory to the Lamb of God!

Therefore, put on the armor of God early in the morning by praying. You will get mighty results from prayer. Let your prayers be real and from your heart, not done out of repetition or ritual. Why? Because God loves a heart that is hungry for Him, a heart that cries out from the depth of the soul, not a rote, memorized prayer that has no passion or emotion attached to it. Our God is a passionate God, and those that worship Him must do so in spirit and in truth.

Prayer is the vehicle by which you are meant to commune with the invisible yet omnipresent God. It is the medium by which your spirit is intended to affect and be affected by the will and purpose of the divine Creator. You are giving God permission to interfere in your affairs. You're allowing God's will to be done over yours, for His will to be done on your portion of earth as it is in His heaven. Prayer is the terrestrial license for celestial interference. The shortest distance between a problem and a solution is the distance between your knees and the floor. Those who kneel before God can stand before anyone.

There are two specific Bible verses about prayer that I have embraced and believe with every fiber of my being. The first is, "If My people who are called by My name will humble themselves, and pray and seek My face, and turn from their wicked ways, then I will hear from heaven, and will forgive their sin and heal their land" (2 Chron. 7:14). The second was spoken by Jesus Himself: "Therefore I say to you, whatever things you ask when you pray, believe that you receive them, and you will have them" (Mark 11:24).

Many are not blessed and their prayers are not answered because they are not giving God priority or permission to interfere in their lives. I understand that there is a season or a period when we simply must wait for God's divine timing to orchestrate itself. However, I also know there is a season that when all else is failing, we simply need to P.U.S.H. (Pray Until Something Happens). We must cry out from the heart like Jacob, who as he wrestled the angel alleged, "I won't let go until you bless me." If your problems haven't stopped, then neither should your prayers. Don't get caught up or bogged down by the details of prayer. Let it come from the depths of your heart and not be superficial. A format I use can be remembered as A.C.T.S. (Adoration, Confession, Thanksgiving, and Supplication). Just keep it real!

If God answers your prayers, He is increasing your faith. If He doesn't, trust that He is training your patience. Praise God for your "not yets" because your "right nows" are not the end of the blessing. Prayer changes things for you or changes you for things. It is a place of miracles! Before miracles are manifested in the physical realm, they go to a place called prayer. Prayer is a great stress reliever because God will listen when nobody else does. What wings are to a bird, and sails to a ship, so is prayer to the soul. However, know that prayer is not a spare wheel that you pull out when you're in trouble; it is a steering wheel that will direct you on the right path throughout your life. How you pray determines what kind of life you live. When you have the boldness to ask God for big things, He will open big doors that might otherwise never open.

Nobody can grow spiritually without a continually developing prayer life. When life is rough, pray; and when life is great, pray. Trust God to answer your prayer and be a constant help in time of need. He's not sleeping or slouching off. In fact, the Bible tells us in 1 Peter 3:12, "For the eyes of the LORD are on the righteous, and His ears are open to their prayers; but the face of the LORD is against those who do evil."

Prayer prevents us from falling into temptation. In the past, if I would go a week without praying, it would increase the appetite of my flesh more than usual, thereby facilitating my fall into temptation. Most of the time, if we're honest with ourselves, when we sin it's because our guard has been lowered due to a weak prayer life. Keep prayer continual and be strengthened so you can resist the fiery darts of the enemy.

ASSISTANCE FOR YOUR RESISTANCE

Another thing I began to do early in my Christian walk that improved my choices and decision making and truly helped me live a more stable life was to actively resist the enemy. First Peter 5:8 says, "Be well balanced (temperate, sober of mind), be vigilant and cautious at all times; for that enemy of yours, the devil, roams around like a lion roaring [in fierce hunger], seeking someone to seize upon and devour" (AMPC). Many in today's church are compromising His Word, while the enemy of our souls stalks us in full force. He is not playing around and neither should we. In fact, in John 10:10 Jesus tells us, "The thief does not come except to steal, and to kill, and to destroy. I have come that they may have life, and that they may have it more abundantly." When you accepted Jesus as your Savior, it was meant for you to be in charge of your mind, emotions, passions, troubles, money, career, desires, and situations. God is in control of His overall perfect will, but He gave us some control too.

We have to let go of some things before the enemy destroys us. It is crucial to let go of things that are gradually killing us even though it feels like letting go of them will kill us. This is when we have to do something no one really likes to do, and that is resist. But we are commanded in James 4:7, "Therefore submit to God. Resist the devil and he will flee from you." It takes very little effort to do what we want, but what happens if what we want is taking us down a dangerous path to destruction? We have to fight and not be so lazy and comfortable.

Resisting the devil is not something you do mildly. We cannot approach the battle casually nor can we compromise God's Word. Our sin causes us to resist God when we should resist the devil. What is it that you specifically need to resist? Is it lust, addiction, unhealthy foods, fear, worry, pride—what? The experience of becoming pure, holy, and strong in the Lord is not a gift like salvation. It takes work and effort.

Salvation is an ACT, but sanctification is a PROCESS. However, it sure is better to resist the enemy and suffer some than to be stuck in a vicious cycle for an entire lifetime. The wilderness and valleys that our poor choices have led us into require our minds to be renewed so that we can make good choices to be delivered and rescued. Staying stuck is definitely not the will of God for our lives.

The things we hold on to and don't give to God keep us restricted and stuck in spiritual and emotional mire. Holding on to things that we are supposed to let go of keeps our lives in a season in which we're no longer supposed to be. We must resist in order to keep moving forward. When you accepted Christ as your Savior, not only did your relationship to Christ change, but your relationship to Satan also changed. Now he really can't stand you and is going to try even harder to lure you to back to your vices and vile ways. You must resist! Keep foremost in mind that no longer are you a slave to sin, as it is written in Romans 6:6: "Knowing this, that our old man was crucified with Him, that the body of sin might be done away with, that we should no longer be slaves of sin." When Satan comes knocking on your door, let him know that you don't work for him anymore. If you know Jesus Christ as your Lord and Savior, you only have one boss, and it's not the devil.

Christian lifestyles are so out of whack these days, with many people living two different lives. Our Saturday nights are so different from our Sunday mornings. I can attest to this because I used to go to church with a hangover from partying the entire night before. Yes, there was a sort of fun and pleasure to it, but in the end, I was not truly satisfied like I am today. Glory to God that I am free today, and there is no better high than abiding in the Most High. Being in His presence is more addictive and satisfying to me because there is nothing this world has that can compete. I come alive in His presence. I am full of life in His presence. I now no longer walk with the spirit of this age, which is passive, self-indulgent, and does not fear God. Romans 6:12 says, "Therefore do not let sin reign in your mortal body, that you should obey it in its lusts." Therefore, if we desire to be cleansed, we must not only submit ourselves to God, but we must also resist that which is evil.

Temptation makes you want things now! When you feel temptation, remember these three words: Stop, Think, and Resist! These three little words have saved me from many headaches, heartaches, and financial disasters. It all starts with the mind. Don't dwell on what is tempting you by rehashing it over and over in your head. I am personally aware of the vicious cycle this can lead to, in which your mind can focus on nothing else! You feel trapped, but resistance is the only way to disrupt those dark forces. Resistance is a vital tool we can use against temptation. To resist is to stand your ground so you don't fall back on bad habits. Sometimes, though, we must resist temptation by running as fast as we can so we don't fall.

Oftentimes the things that make us better Christians don't make us feel good. Change and gradual transformation calls us to discomfort, pain, and humility. However, the long-term results are always rewarding, beneficial, and worthwhile. Remember that! Sometimes it takes time to develop sufficient resistance to quash the attack. I encourage you to keep resisting and declaring the blood of Jesus over your life. He destroyed the enemy and conquered death. Believe that God's got you and that He's working it all for your good. Remain dependent on your Savior and Lord!

3

WALKING IN THE FEAR OF THE LORD

Therefore, since we are receiving a kingdom
which cannot be shaken, let us have grace,
by which we may serve God acceptably
with reverence and godly fear.

—HEBREWS 12:28

BECAUSE MANY PEOPLE know they can sin and will be
forgiven if they ask for it, they live to commit rather
than to correct. They prefer to hear about God's love
and mercy than His wrath. Could this be why Christians
are so passive in their walk or service? Our God is a God of
righteousness and justice, a consuming fire, but most prefer
to see Him as one of "no hell" existence. It's too burdensome
for them to think that a God of love would also have wrath,
so they don't understand the need to fear Him.

Well, God is serious about producing the change in
our lives that will glorify Him and cause us to rise higher.
Salvation is not the climax of Christianity. God desires
for us to produce fruit and mature spiritually. Every great
leap forward in your life comes after you have made a
clear decision of some kind. Choosing to walk in the fear

of the Lord is no different, especially since His Word says, "Therefore, my beloved, as you have always obeyed, not as in my presence only, but now much more in my absence, work out your own salvation with *fear* and trembling" (Phil. 2:12, emphasis added).

Before we go deeper into this chapter, let me explain what it means to walk in the fear of the Lord. Walking in the fear of the Lord is living with a profound respect and reverence for Him; not necessarily a terrifying thing, but having a desire to not go against or violate because you're paying close attention to Him. To further clarify, it is being afraid to offend God in any way and get so deep in sin that you won't obtain forgiveness. Why? Because in Hebrews 10:30–31 it says, "For we know him who said, 'It is mine to avenge; I will repay,' and again, 'The Lord will judge his people.' It is a dreadful thing to fall into the hands of the living God" (NIV).

You may wonder, "Are you saying He won't forgive me, Pastor Hery?" Yes, He will forgive you, but only if you are really serious about your repentance. Look what the Word of God says in these couple of verses beginning with Hebrews 10:26–27: "For if we sin willfully after we have received the knowledge of the truth, there no longer remains a sacrifice for sins, but a certain *fearful* expectation of judgment, and fiery indignation which will devour the adversaries" (emphasis added). Then in Matthew 10:28, "Do not be afraid of those who kill the body but cannot kill the soul. Rather, be afraid of the One who can destroy both soul and body in hell" (NIV). I don't know about you, but I would rather not take any chances playing with sin.

THE IMPORTANCE OF WALKING IN THE FEAR OF THE LORD

We derive many benefits when we choose to walk in the fear of the Lord. For one, it brings knowledge. Proverbs 1:7

tells us that "The fear of the Lord is the beginning of knowledge, but fools despise wisdom and instruction." We are to live Spirit-led, not self-driven. How many times have you heard the phrase, "Follow your heart"? Well, better not leave the mind behind!

We can also count on wisdom being part of the blessings when we walk in the fear of the Lord. The Word says in Psalm 111:10, "The fear of the LORD is the beginning of wisdom; all who follow his precepts have good understanding. To Him belongs eternal praise" (NIV). Not fearing the Lord will lead to ignorance and blindness as to heavenly treasures. Don't look for wisdom in your circumstance; instead, ask God for wisdom about your circumstance.

Walking in the fear of the Lord helps us to hate evil. We then walk in humility and hate what God hates. Proverbs 8:13 tells us, "To fear the LORD is to hate evil; I hate pride and arrogance, evil behavior and perverse speech." We reap the opposite effect when we flirt with evil or sin and then get corrupted or entangled by it. Sometimes we even get self-righteous and proud because we believe our sin is not as bad as the sin of another. I love how the Reverend Billy Graham put it: "It's the Holy Spirit's job to convict, God's job to judge, and my job to love."[1] What a powerful clarification of the gospel!

Another benefit of walking in the fear of the Lord is that it helps us depart from evil. In other words, it helps us resist temptation and the devil's fiery darts. Proverbs 16:6 says, "Through love and faithfulness sin is atoned for; through the fear of the LORD evil is avoided" (NIV). Rest assured that the opposite action—that is, not being motivated to repent of our sins or failing to turn to God to work out our salvation—will lead to evil.

Do you want to live longer? Well, walking in the fear of the Lord will extend the days of your life. Proverbs 10:27 tells us, "The fear of the LORD adds length to life, but the years of the wicked are cut short" (NIV). The opposite effect is dying prematurely because of the consequences of sin. Sin is so not worth it! It will keep you longer than you want to stay and cost you more than you want to pay...not to mention age you prematurely.

Many of us walk with our shoulders down because of a poor self-image and negative self-esteem. Walking in the fear of the Lord helps us live with confidence. We don't need another self-help book, though I know some are helpful. We just have to walk in the fear of the Lord. "Whoever fears the LORD has a secure fortress, and for their children it will be a refuge" (Prov. 14:26, NIV). To do the opposite is to not really engage the assurance and confidence salvation truly brings. May I ask you to really ponder this question: How many of you want the mercy of God upon you and your children? Unless you are completely heartless or in denial, your answer will be a resounding "I do!" I would like you to embrace this Bible verse: "But from everlasting to everlasting the LORD's love is with those who fear him, and his righteousness with their children's children—with those who keep his covenant and remember to obey his precepts" (Ps. 103:17–18, NIV). Wow! What a wonderful promise we and our children have when we choose to walk fearing the almighty Creator of the universe.

Another benefit of walking in the fear of the Lord is that it helps us build up our humility and rewards us with riches. Proverbs 22:4 says, "Humility is the fear of the LORD; its wages are riches and honor and life" (NIV). I'm convinced that humility pays higher dividends than pride. Pride destroys, brings distance to relationships, and does not allow Jesus to fully live and reveal Himself in the manner He desires. Humility comes by surrendering your will to God, and that ultimately brings us the best results. Humility is a great medicine for any relationship! You will only go as far as your humility will allow you. I like to remind people that no matter how big your house is, how recent a model your car is, or how impressive your bank account is, our graves will always be the same size. Stay humble, my friend!

Lastly, if we choose to walk in the fear of the Lord, it helps us live blessed.

Psalm 128:1 says, "Blessed are all who fear the LORD, who walk in obedience to him" (NIV). Another supportive verse is Psalm 112:1, "Praise the LORD. Blessed are those who fear the LORD, who find great delight in His commands" (NIV).

In conclusion, there are so many benefits to walking in the fear of the Lord that we and our families cannot afford to take the chance of living any other way. This Bible verse from the wisest man that ever lived, King Solomon, summarizes it all: "Now all has been heard; here is the conclusion of the matter: fear God and keep his commandments, for this is the duty of all mankind" (Eccles. 12:13).

DEVELOPING THE FEAR OF THE LORD

You're probably saying, "Pastor Hery, I get you, but how do I develop the fear of the Lord?" Well, for one you need to hear the Word of God. Romans 10:17 says, "Consequently, faith comes from hearing the message, and the message is heard through the word about Christ" (NIV). I sometimes hear people say they don't need to go to church to hear the Word. Well, aside from the fact that God wants "like faiths" to congregate, what better way is there to hear it? Where else can you get such a profound encounter other than being in His presence with like-minded individuals?

Another obvious way to develop the fear of the Lord is by reading and studying the Word of God. The Book of Psalms, which is my personal favorite, is loaded with scriptures on the fear of the Lord. Do you want God to talk to you? Raise up your Bible and say, "Lord, please talk to me." The Bible is the unadulterated Word of God because it was "God-breathed," and God does not have bad breath! I know I'm being facetious, but the fact of the matter is you are either in the Word being conformed to the image of Jesus Christ or you are in the world being squeezed into its mold. Understand that the Bible is not just for your information, but for your transformation. I don't understand all of it myself, but what I do understand has required me to change how I live.

A third way to develop the fear of the Lord is by walking in balance with the Word of God. This means in ALL aspects of our being, living fit in the spirit, soul, and body. Why? Because when we do so, the enemy of our soul will have a tougher time getting to us. One of my favorite verses is 1 Peter 5:8, which says, "Be alert and of sober mind. Your enemy the devil prowls around like a roaring lion looking for someone to devour" (NIV).

Live in such a way that you are secure, stable, and relatable. The almighty God lives in you; therefore, you have nothing to prove and nothing to hide. Being a fanatic or an extremist may possibly shut the door on somebody that needs the love and compassion, yet authenticity, of Jesus Christ. I've come across people who when simply asked "Good morning, sir. How are you?" will respond with "I am blessed and highly favored. Jesus reigns and I praise His mighty name." That just raises the hair on the back of neck, and my initial response is to tell them, "Well, tell me something I don't know." But I just say, "Good for you," and walk away knowing that I will think twice before asking them next time. Folks, our feet are still touching the soil of the earth. I'm all for enthusiasm and a positive attitude, but can we also just be real, relatable, and balanced?

A fourth way of developing the fear of the Lord is by truly repenting, which will lead to obedience (fear and trembling that comes of our salvation). The evidence of repentance may be gradual or it can be an immediate change. Too many people are living without the fear of the Lord and in a cycle of repetitive sinning without a desire to change. Change is not change until there is genuine transformation. Second Corinthians 7:1 reads, "Therefore, since we have these promises, dear friends, let us purify ourselves from everything that contaminates body and spirit, perfecting holiness out of reverence for God" (NIV). Many people in the church today have not really repented. They "know" the Word, but don't "DO" the Word. May God have mercy on their souls. Repentance is the soil in which forgiveness flourishes. I hear people wanting a revival this and a revival that, but revival really starts with you!

Lastly, if you want to develop the fear of the Lord, you need to be praying for the Spirit of God to place that fear of the Lord in your soul. Prayer may not always change your circumstances, but it will always change you. Therefore, go for it and ask God the Father anyway. I love what Jesus said in Mark 11:24: "Therefore I tell you, whatever you ask for in prayer, believe that you have received it, and it will be yours" (NIV).

We will always have trouble in this world, and prayer will always be necessary because a prayerless Christian is a powerless Christian. Until you recognize that life is war, you cannot know what prayer is truly for. I encourage you to keep the faith even if your prayers are not being answered. You have to praise and thank God anyway for your "not yets" because your "right nows" are not necessarily the end of the blessing. Eventually when you pray, especially for something such as the fear of the Lord being placed in you, it will move the hands of the God who rules the world.

4

DYING TO SELF IN ORDER TO LIVE

Then [Jesus] said to them all: "Whoever *wants*
to be my disciple must *deny* themselves and
take up their cross daily and *follow* me. For
whoever wants to save their life will lose it, but
whoever loses their life for me will save it."
—LUKE 9:23–24, NIV, EMPHASIS ADDED

I N THE BIBLE verse above, make note of the four words written in italics. They are the foundation of this chapter. This verse is the crux of Christianity because it strikes a death blow to the self-centeredness, egocentricity, and the ultra-selfishness in which humans indulge.

First, this chapter is for those who WANT to get closer to Jesus Christ. This is not an obligation; it's only for those who truly want it. If you are not yet at that point in your walk, then maybe this chapter isn't for you, because it will require you to examine yourself and rise up. Jesus doesn't force anyone to do anything. This chapter is for those who WANT God's best despite the fact that it won't come easily.

You will next notice the word DENY, which is so difficult—but not impossible—to do. Denying the flesh is a lifetime process and will bring life to your soul, but keep in mind that no true sacrifice is fun.

If you are still reading and interested, you'll see the next thing that is required of you is to TAKE UP your cross. The Word promises us in 1 Corinthians 10:13, "No temptation has overtaken [seized] you except such as is common to man; but God is faithful, who will not allow you to be tempted beyond what you are able, but with the temptation will also make the way of escape, that you may be able to bear it." Therefore, the cross you carry is just perfect for you. It's not too easy nor too difficult—it's just right.

Lastly, after you've made the choice to WANT this, DENY self, and TAKE UP your cross, you are now in a position to FOLLOW Jesus. You are His disciple, not just someone who has a casual and passive relationship with Him. I will elaborate further on these four terms later in the chapter.

In John 7:37 (NIV), Jesus calls forth he "who is thirsty" (or hungry for more). This emphasizes that His Word is not for everyone; only for those who WANT it! You may be saying, "Pastor Hery, I'm ready for this—give me Jesus!" While I like your enthusiasm, let me ask you, "Are you willing to suffer and die if necessary?" Thank God those of us in the United States don't experience an overwhelming cross as do Christians in other countries. Thank God for the foundation of this country and the praying people who live in it. Christianity is not something to "try on" like a dress or something to be done your way; it's living your life His way.

We have to understand that as long as "self" is in control, God can't have His way in us. We have to DENY ourselves so that He can get the ultimate glory and our lives will have true life in them. The fact that most people merely exist and don't thrive is indicative that they are losing precious days of their lives that could have been lived with more peace and joy. When we deny ourselves, or die to self, it is not a thing we do only once. It will be more of a constant dying as Jesus helps us remove unnecessary things inside us that bog down our journey. We will be faced with many decisions throughout our day that will require a choice to deny self.

The Bible says in Proverbs 16:25, "There is a way that appears to be right, but in the end it leads to death" (NIV). Why do we hesitate to die for Christ, who brings us life, when living for self only brings us death? Many want the blessings and fulfillment but are not willing to even temporarily (not forever) suffer and crucify the flesh. As it is written in Galatians 5:24–25, "Those who belong to Christ Jesus have crucified the flesh [sinful nature] with its passions and desires. Since we live by the Spirit, let us keep in step with the Spirit" (NIV). Real freedom comes from resisting the enemy and dying to our selfish will. It's not easy, but it is possible with the power of Jesus Christ living within us.

Many people have this misconception that dying to self makes a person miserable, but the fact of the matter is that refusing to die to self is what really makes one miserable. In self there is death, but in Christ there is life. This is why we see so many people who are lifeless, restless, stressed, anxious, unhappy, and depressed. As it is written in John 6:63, "The Spirit gives life; the flesh counts for nothing. The words I have spoken to you—they are full of the Spirit and life" (NIV). Yes, my brother or sister, the Spirit of God gives life, and it comes when we choose to walk in His will rather than our dead-end way. There is no resurrection without death!

Let me ask you another question: Is your relationship with God one of "What's in it for me," or "What can I do for Him?" The latter relationship is true discipleship (Christianity) and everything else is basically lip service or religion (bondage). If this present life is important to you, then you will do all you can to protect it. You will stay in your comfort and safety zone and not risk anything. Listen, nothing material, familial, financial or any other kind of earthly thing can compare to eternity. The faster we submit to His will, the more at peace and joyful we will be. The devil can't stop you, and he can't do a thing with you unless God allows him to. People give him way too much credit. The biggest problem is not the devil but our flesh.

BREAKING DOWN FURTHER THE OPENING BIBLE VERSE

To Christians, to DENY ourselves means to submit to the will of God in everything! Even when it hurts; even when you don't want to; even when that evil, sinful pleasure is what you desire; even when you get ridiculed; even if it means losing some worldly friends, a questionable job, or your possessions (in summary, people or things that lean toward the sinful nature). We need to deny our sinful nature so that our redeemed nature can emerge and shine. This is not accomplished by self-effort but a choice in the sanctification process on which we've embarked.

In Romans 12:1-2 it says, "Therefore, I urge you, brothers and sisters, in view of God's mercy, to offer your bodies as a living sacrifice, holy and pleasing to God—this is your true and proper worship. Do not conform to the pattern of this world, but be transformed by the renewing of your mind. Then you will be able to test and approve what God's will is—his good, pleasing and perfect will" (NIV). This is not going to be easy or fun, as discipline requires us to make uncomfortable-in-the-flesh decisions, but it will comfort our souls. Hebrews 12:11 explains it better: "No discipline seems pleasant at the time, but painful. Later on, however, it produces a harvest of righteousness and peace for those who have been trained by it" (NIV). Many of us want to live for self instead of how God desires, and thus the cross becomes heavier than necessary.

I want to suggest that you count the cost before you dive into that sinful act of pleasure, because again, it will take you further than you want to go, keep you longer than you want to stay, and cost you more than you want to pay. Rehearse the consequences; to experience the abundance of a spiritual spring, it is necessary to first embrace the death of winter. Have the mind-set that what you want no longer matters. Jesus gave Himself to you, so choose to give yourself to Him.

To take up the cross means you now carry your instrument of death because you have died to yourself and no longer live for your own interests, desires, and pleasures; you must do what He wills. Christ now lives in you, and your choices are to be based on His will. Obviously, it is not a physical death but an ALL IN sacrifice of self to do His will. I like how the Apostle Paul puts it in Galatians 2:20: "I have been crucified with Christ and I no longer live, but Christ lives in me. The life I now live in the body, I live by faith in the Son of God, who loved me and gave himself for me" (NIV).

For me personally, when I've chosen to follow God, it hasn't always made sense, but things have worked out well. When I've chosen to disobey God and follow my own plan, it seemed to make sense in the moment, but things didn't work out well. I am convinced that there won't be any crown-bearers in heaven that weren't cross-bearers down here on earth.

To follow Christ does not mean merely to say a prayer or walk down an aisle or sign a card and become a Christian. Being followers of Jesus Christ means that we learn what His will is and we do it. The determination to give our lives to God's service is called "repentance," and many are not His disciples because they don't totally sacrifice. There is an old saying that says becoming a Christian is free, but being a Christian will cost you everything. In summary, it means giving and dedicating your whole life to God.

But what is it about you that must die? Well, Christ died so that we could live, and the thing is, He expects the same from us—for us to live a crucified life. You may think, "Well, Pastor Hery, I'm not sure I want to do this. It sounds tough and will cost me too much." Rest assured, the alternative will cost you more! As the Word of God indicates in Romans 8:6, "For to be carnally minded is death, but to be spiritually minded is life and peace." I know you desire for your soul to be filled with life, and I'm counting on the fact that you want to please God as well. Well, walking in the flesh won't allow you to do that. According to Romans 8:8, "Those who are in the flesh [controlled by the sinful nature] cannot please God." Furthermore, Romans 8:13 says, "For if you live according to the flesh [sinful nature] you will die; but if by the Spirit you put to death the deeds of the body, you will live." Do you desire life, or a progressive collapse and ultimate breakdown?

If a person holds their life so dear that they want to live only to please themselves, do their own will, and accomplish their own purposes rather than denying self and serving God, that person will, in the end, lose his life eternally. People have to understand that by dying, they will live! How many heartbreaks and headaches must you endure before you realize that the "good life" comes by living for Jesus Christ? Die to self and stop your struggle! Sin cannot be negotiated or tamed. You have to die to self by asking God to cut you open and remove all the impurities that are keeping you entangled in sin. The main reason we fear the need to go under the knife of "The Great Physician" is giving up control. But Jesus wants you to surrender and trust Him. So answer me this: who is going to be your master?

Most people live with areas of their souls reserved solely to exercise control rather than to surrender. But as long as they keep repeating this behavior, their lives will remain a battleground for the enemy. The act of surrender must be a deliberate act of our will. God is saying, "Give this to Me, get My rest, and let Me finish this work in you." We have one shot at life, and we can either live it for the Lord or live it for ourselves. We are either resting our souls in His almighty hands or in our own. The Christian walk as Jesus designed it is choosing death or life on a daily basis. Take the jump and be "ALL IN!"

WHAT HAPPENS WHEN YOU CRUCIFY THE FLESH?

1. THERE IS NEW LIFE AND A NEW COMMITMENT TO GOD.

When we surrender to the new creation of self, we begin to change, transform, and mature. Please note that our personality doesn't change, but our character, behavior, and conduct does. We were once controlled by the sinful nature but now we have chosen to have Jesus live within us. We now do not operate on our own strength and begin to show fruit. It is no longer all about us (OUR interests, behaviors, pleasures, and desires). Jesus is now our Lord and Master, not just our Savior. Control has been surrendered! Giving up control is one of the most liberating things we can do because when we give up control, God assumes full responsibility for our needs.

2. We can find rest and peace for our souls.

Life can be overwhelming at times and can even fracture you. You won't always feel strong. Neither did Jesus—but He always recognized and went to His source! The ways we now handle daily pressure, issues, burdens, and concerns will change. Difficulties may continue, but we will never be crushed by them. Peace exists! Our lives rest BEST in Him because His peace is perfect!

3. We can live with power!

God's almighty resurrected power that lifted Jesus from the grave now lives in us. We can do great and mighty things because authority and dominion have been restored to us by the sacrifice at the cross. Yet many rely on self-strength, intellect, and ability, which doesn't lead to much, especially in eternity. Jesus was determined, committed, and connected to the Source. How foolish to think we can do all these things without connecting to the Source.

4. We can live with victory over sin.

The power of God is evident when He is able to free us from bondage, entanglement, and self. Freedom can only be accomplished by crucifying our flesh (denying the self). We need to realize that we walk around with an almighty God inside of us. We can now surrender the fight rather than fight it and fail. Don't beat yourself up when you fall or, worse yet, actively choose to sin. Simply turn to Jesus and repent! Sheep may slip into the mud, but pigs stay in the mud. There is nothing Satan can throw your way that Jesus cannot defeat. Stop living with an anesthetized soul, and make a conscious choice to live for Him.

5. We can live with stability, security, and self-confidence.

Life is filled with ups and downs, but your life doesn't have to be a roller coaster of victory and defeat. When we allow God to live through us, our souls are not governed by circumstances but by the One. Our life is a tree that must be planted or grounded to prosper. Stop moving it around so frequently. Allow it to stay in God. We have to make this decision to deny ourselves continually, not just as a one-time thing. In other words, it's not necessarily what you rebelliously believe, but how you obey (choice) His Word that determines your divine destiny.

We have to recognize our weaknesses and inadequacies and ask God to help us win. Christians who have surrendered to Jesus realize they can't live life on their own. The old self can never be improved enough; it just needs to be CRUCIFIED. Jesus emptied Himself, giving His ALL for you so you can now live for Him. Our Lord did not ask us to give up the things of earth but to exchange them for even better things!

Let the Spirit of God "slay and kill" the things your old self still wants to keep but your new self knows are not good for your journey. Be liberated in Jesus's name! Let Him transform what is ugly into something lovely, weakness into strength, and what has brought death to your soul to now bring it life. Let the Spirit of God gently inspire you to stop living half-heartedly and be "ALL IN" for Him. Remember, there is no living unless there is dying!

PART 2

GROWING IN LOVE

PART 2

GROWING IN LOVE

5

FORGET THE PAST AND EMBRACE THE NEW

Forget the former things; do not dwell on
the past. See, I am doing a new thing!
—ISAIAH 43:18–19, NIV

S I MENTIONED in Chapter 2, life is about choices and decisions. You will have many situations in your life when it will be your choice whether to dwell or move forward. The choice is yours. You can either choose to let the hurts, wounds, and pains from your past continue to strangle and paralyze you, or you can choose to say enough is enough and give God the green light to free you from the bad things from your past that haunt you. His power and His help are there for you if you are willing to take His hand and allow Him to bring you up out of it!

Too many Christians are so bound up in their past that they cannot live in the present! Before you can really start to move forward in your divine walk, calling, purpose, and destiny with the Lord, you will first have to learn how to fully let your past go. Many people get stalled well beyond a reasonable time of healing over their broken marriage; shattered dreams; having been the victim of a crime or physical, verbal, or sexual abuse; the death of a close loved one; loss of a job or other financial disaster; or any other crisis that can leave a scar on the soul. God is saying, "Don't dwell on it any longer; for I have plans to restore you and bring in something new. I'm your Strength and your Refuge; put your trust in Me."

I am here to encourage you today that there is life after breakups and heartaches. The past should be left in the past; otherwise it can destroy your future. Live life for what tomorrow has to offer, not for what yesterday has taken away.

I love what the Apostle Paul wrote in Philippians 3:12–14:

> Not that I have already attained, or am already perfected; but I press on, that I may lay hold of that for which Christ Jesus has also laid hold of me. Brethren, I do not count myself to have apprehended; but one thing I do, forgetting those things which are behind and reaching forward to those things which are ahead, I press toward the goal for the prize of the upward call of God in Christ Jesus.

In other words, God will do His part in helping us forget the past (not dwell over it), but we have to do our part by "pressing" toward our goal with a forward thinking mind-set.

Let me ask you a question: What are you carrying and dragging around that is preventing you from having the abundant life Jesus died for you to have? Repeatedly looking back is going to hinder God from doing His new blessing in your life. How can the new come when the old is still intact? How can healing occur if we lack faith that God can heal our wounds? In Luke 9:62 Jesus said to a man who wanted to go back to his past, "No one, having put his hand to the plow, and looking back, is fit for the kingdom of God." My friend, don't try to figure it out. Instead, faith it out!

The Lord doesn't want your peace disturbed. He wants you to trust Him for your future. You don't have to be some sort of scientific genius and try to figure it all out. You're a saint in the making, a child of God, and His blessings come to you with no sorrow. When you let go in order to move on, it requires you to trust the wonder-working power of the Healer of your Soul. I don't know how He does it, but I know He restores if you surrender your ALL to Him. Your life is not over—there is always hope in Him. He still has plans for you. First Corinthians 2:9 should inspire you to strengthen your belief: "No eye has seen, no ear has heard, and no mind has imagined what God has prepared for those who love him" (NLT). Do you love Him? If so, then you qualify for miraculous impromptu bursts of new living that will bring tremendous joy to your soul. You qualify to have a life of freedom in your soul.

The better question is, can you move forward and resist the urge to go or look back? This question refers to regression in both physical and mental capacities. Many of us have been healed, liberated, and delivered by the almighty God, but our minds have not been convinced. We are playing "catch up" while God is in a position to bless us beyond measure. He's probably saying, "My child, My child, I want to bless you, but you are holding Me back."

There is an internal part of us that dies when we decide to "go back" after God has already done His work. There is no provision or prosperity of the soul. We get off track from the purpose that will lead us to the destiny that God is creating for us. Prayers are hindered, blessings are delayed, and we have to start over. The calendar starts anew every year, but that does not mean your past situation has to keep starting over or even continuing. Stop taking forbidden steps or shortcuts to escape your pain! Choose right and focus on healing while moving forward.

You have the choice to be either dependent on God or self-sufficient. Understand that before a breakthrough, a blessing, or a release of the supernatural, something will always come against your mind and try to get you battle weary. Keep fighting the good fight of faith! Keep depending on the Lord's strength and power. The development of your very character depends on your decision.

You will need to be determined to forget the past and to stay focused on the life He wants to give you. Prayer and fasting obviously will help, but your determination is what will prevail! I believe that determination plus trusting in God equals complete healing! This means forgiving yourself and others. This means surrendering your resentment or ill feelings to the cross, because Jesus died so you don't have to carry those burdens any longer.

It's not about totally forgetting everything in the past. We actually learn from the past, and we are to remember God's work in our lives; those things help us move forward. But we must never let the past stop us from running the race. There is no veering off track in this race, no deciding to quit serving God and stop focusing on knowing Jesus further. It is not healthy to drag dead things into a future full of life. It is not prudent to be mentally engaged in things that steal your peace, joy, and vitality. You owe it to yourself and your loved ones to stop dwelling on things of the past and start living. The next time the devil reminds you of the past, remind him of his future.

In conclusion, you must learn how to let go, so you can go on. You must learn to control those hindering thoughts from your past before you can start to proceed full steam ahead in your walk and calling for the Lord. If you don't learn how to fully let go of your past, you will stay stuck right where you are and never fully accomplish everything that God has in store for you in this life. It's like the blind spot when you're driving your car. Each of us has a blind spot in life, but we also have a sweet spot that comes from above. Focusing on one will hinder your destiny, while focusing on the other will bring it to fruition. The one you feed will grow, and the one you don't, like anything else, will die. Where will your thoughts go? Which will you feed? I believe this will be a glorious year for those who listen, believe, adjust, and persevere![1]

from your past before you can start to proceed full steam ahead in your walk and calling for the Lord. If you don't learn how to fully let go of your past, you will stay stuck right where you are and never fully accomplish everything that God has in store for you in this life. It's like the blind spot when you're driving your car. Each of us has a blind spot in life, but we also have a sweet spot that comes from above. Focusing on one will hinder your destiny, while focusing on the other will bring it to fruition. The one you feed will grow, and the one you don't, like anything else, will die. Where will your thoughts go? Which will you feed? I believe this will be a glorious year for those who listen, believe, adjust, and persevere."

6

HEALING THE SOUL FROM A ROMANTIC PAST

Though you have made me see troubles, many and
bitter, you will restore my life again; from the
depths of the earth you will again bring me up.

—PSALM 71:20, NIV

ONE OF THE most difficult and heart-challenging
things to conquer in life is getting over a failed
romantic relationship. It doesn't matter if it's a
marriage gone sour because of infidelity, abuse, or simply
quitting, or a toxic relationship going nowhere. You have
simply realized that the person can stay in your heart, just
not in your life. You've parted ways, but now what? How
do you get over these thoughts that seem to consume you?

Trying to forget someone you loved is like trying to
remember someone you never knew. It seems impossible,
but with your determination and God's healing, you will
recover. It may not be in a day, but you will heal by day by
day. When will you fully heal? Well, that depends on YOU.
You can drag it out by prolonging the full healing process,
or you can make a decision to let go. It might feel like

you're bleeding internally, but trust that you will survive. Tough it out certain in the knowledge that you can do ALL things through Christ. Just keep in mind that God doesn't operate on your timetable. He's never in a hurry, but He's always right. So it will require you to trust and be patient in the healing process.

I had to overcome a tainted love relationship that had me in bondage. This was the most difficult obstacle I ever had to face. The worst part was the mental entanglement and confusion after the initial breakup. I've never done drugs, so I'm not sure how an addict feels as they experience withdrawals, but mine were intensely uncomfortable. The vice I had in my life because of this obsession almost took my purpose and my life. It was an evil assignment from the enemy to trap me and alter my God-given destiny with this disharmonious relationship. But praise God for His will to rule in my life!

It took years to heal, mainly because I kept making stupid choices to hang on to something that was never meant to be. Like trying to build a puzzle with missing pieces, it simply wasn't going to happen. But by the grace of God and my determination to do what is right, I was able to overcome. However, I had to get used to living out of my comfort zone until it actually became comfortable. I had to close many doors, and that's what you will need to do if you desire to welcome the new. That's what you will need to do to move forward. That's what you will need to do to become whole again. Understand that your "nEXt" will have nothing to do with your "EX."

It is so unfair to your present or even potential mate to have them deal with just part of you and not all of you. Be upfront and let them know about your mind-set now and definitely before you get married! Anything causing disorder in your present that stems from someone in your past or from someone still hanging around today has to be released. Getting over a painful experience is much like crossing the monkey bars in the playground—you have to let go of one rung in order to move forward to the next. Dead things must be buried; if not, they'll ferment into decay and disease.

Much like a frozen PC, we can use these three steps to help us move on: "CTRL + ALT + DEL." For us that would translate to "control yourself, look for an alternative solution, and delete toxic romantic relationships." Stop pressing replay on the things that need to be deleted from your life. What you are willing to walk away from determines what God will bring you. If you love him or her but it's wrong and out of order, you have to let them go! When you insist on still hanging on or trying to take someone that is not yours—that is, not given to you by God—He will take something that He did give you. Don't complain when the consequences, hurt, and pain become destructive.

You dug yourself into this unnecessary hole and now you need to cut all ties with that person. If you release your hold on that situation, God will place stepping-stones so you can climb out of that hole. It requires time, trust in God's miraculous process, and you stopping the further "digging" such as any communication, rehashing, occasional coffee outings, booty calls, makeout sessions, looking them up on social media, and talking about them. Every time you give in to any of these, you are digging deeper instead of healing and rising to the surface. You want to be whole for the next relationship and not fractional. An "EX" should mean thank you for the Experience, our time now has Expired, so now Exit from my life.

Partially hanging on to something that was never meant to be is a disservice to yourself and the future dynamic person God is preparing for you. He won't give them to you until you stop looking back! Sometimes it's not that you are necessarily afraid of letting go, but you're just afraid of accepting that fact that it's gone! Your history is not your destiny. Hear me clearly: the best way to get over your past is to build a new one. Find some new faces to familiarize yourself with. Yesterday has already proven itself unworthy; therefore, why go back today to fail again with yesterday and be more miserable in your tomorrow?

If you know a relationship is over, don't keep starting it over! Stop picking up what God has told you to put down. You are praying for your heart to heal, but you won't leave the hurtful situation. You have to take the first step in letting go, and God will do the rest. New beginnings always start with the ending of something old; don't force what doesn't fit your life any longer.

I'm hoping this chapter will help someone avoid the unnecessary trappings of a past relationship that was not meant to be. Some people even know that it's wrong and will bring future havoc, yet they won't let go for whatever odd reason. Life is too short to be going around in circles and repeatedly starting over. Spiritual blindness has paralyzed many! We hurt and cry from broken romantic relationships, but sometimes the best things that happen to us are the things that *don't* happen because they weren't meant to be. Unfortunately, before things fall into place they may have to fall apart! Let me encourage you, reader—there is life after heartbreak. How much life is up to you. Life didn't begin with that person and it doesn't end with them either. Hurt, heal, and move on. When will you know you've healed? You are healed when you still have the memory but not the pain attached to it.

There will come a day when you realize that turning the page is the best feeling in the world because you recognize that there is so much more to your book of life than the page on which you were stuck. Wandering in the wilderness or returning to Egypt (your closed-door past) will keep you from getting to the Promised Land that comes only by moving forward and trusting in God's provision. If your destiny was in Egypt, the Red Sea would have never merged together behind you!

Don't try to understand everything, because some things are not meant to be understood but simply accepted. There is a difference between giving up and letting go. In a healthy relationship, you commit and fight for it, while in unhealthy ones, you simply have to move on. It's better to suffer a few months without them than to be stuck for a multiple of wasted years in a relationship not meant to be. What a drag! It will gradually suck the peace, joy, and life out of you. Stop dragging around dead weight that belongs in the grave! Release it and live!

Stop trying to repair your heart by giving it back to the hands that broke it. It may hurt to let go, but sometimes it hurts even more to hold on. Please stop asking God to take you "forward" when you're in love with your "backward." Sundays, New Years, and sunrises are God's reminders to us that He is all about the new. No matter what you are going through right now, understand that life goes on. If God has given us His own Son, surely He will not do anything to hurt us. God is sovereign. He knows what is best for us. Everything related to us has been prepared by our Father. We should simply pray, "Lord, have Your way. I simply want what You want for me! I leave everything entirely in Your hands." Then give Him the controls, be patient in the waiting process, and watch God come to your rescue.

No matter what you're going through, there is no pit so deep that God can't reach in and get you out. Are you running toward somebody you should be running from and thereby running from the God you should be running toward? God has so much to give you and wants to do so much in your life; don't choose instead to eat the crumbs of the benevolence of other people and miss your opportunity to be blessed by a God who waits up all night for His son or His daughter to come home.

Why go back and open a door that God prompted you to close? Remember you closed the door because you realized that the person really didn't care about you in the first place, or you saw something that told your soul it simply was not meant to be. At times you will miss them, but you have to stay true to reality. Don't live on the potential of the relationship but for what it actually brought forth (the reality of it).

God wants to turn your memories of the past into your hope for the future. You know you are on the right track when you become uninterested in looking back. Our Creator is a God who recycles, restores, and replenishes! Don't give up! What's coming is better than what has been! Besides, you don't live there anymore, and not everyone can go where you're going. Understand that three words sum up life: "It Goes On." Therefore, let bygones be bygones!

So you're single now with no courtship relationship. You might be saying, "Pastor Hery, you've provided a lot of info, but no actual techniques. How do I move on? What do I do?" I'll come to that shortly, but in your singleness, choose to be happy, be holy, and maximize yourself! Nobody wants to begin a new relationship with a fragmented person. Your happiness does not come from a person but from a deep-rooted relationship with Jesus Christ. If you live so that your happiness depends on a mate, you may be single your entire life! God is a jealous

God—He wants no idol or, indeed, anything to come before Him. We pray for God to resurrect situations that are dead and that He is trying to bury, but God wants us to put Him first and walk in right standing with Him. Some people simply need to be LET GO because they distance us from having a deeper relationship with God.

LETTING GO OF A TOXIC ROMANTIC RELATIONSHIP

Just because you have a past with someone, this does not mean you should have a future with them. Sometimes old relationships are blocking the new, and some are so toxic to your future that they will destroy all the blessings for which you are praying and expecting. Some romantic relationships simply need to receive an eviction notice. Anyone in your life who is holding you back, stressing you out, and literally trying to kill your destiny must have your permission to remain part of your life. Some people will leave on their own, but others you will have to KICK OUT!

You don't even need to say a word when letting go in many situations. Stern actions show you're serious and ready for your new life. So, stop expecting closure to always mean that something needs to be spoken by you or heard by them. "Oh, Pastor Hery, I just want to have some closure with them." Why? If the signs have been obvious and all around this relationship, closure doesn't need words. Why should it have to be audible when it's been visible for so long? Closure is not always about something needing to be said, but rather us needing to open our eyes. If it was truly love, they wouldn't have promised; they would have committed. When it's real love and divinely orchestrated, it will have peace, it will flow, and you will know!

Regardless of your approach, allow me to help you here by providing you with five ways to let go so you can move on:

1. Close doors gently (no need to create any drama; plus, it shows you mean business).

2. Forgive.

3. Leave with integrity (have class and take care of your financial responsibilities).

4. Create a plan of action (NO texts, calls, e-mails, "booty calls," or contact whatsoever). Exception: If you have children with them, let your planned talks be about the children.

5. Give yourself six months to heal and seek God's presence (no dating at all).

TAIL-END HEALING TIPS

The hardest part of any battle, whether it's losing five pounds, getting over an addiction, or healing from a relationship, is the end. The person is gone and you don't want them back, but the memories still haunt you, as do the "what if's" and the "could've and should've." Here are ten tips to help you get over this stubborn plateau that can often be difficult to master:

1. See the NEW coming (you being healed and speaking words of life by faith). Keeping your mind in the past is a huge obstacle to moving forward. It causes your spirit to drag and will drain you of your joy. Understand, my brother or sister, that God never gives back what He took away. Especially if it was not meant to be. The enemy's evil assignment appears wonderful,

but it's a trap! He comes to DESTROY you, STEAL your purpose, and maybe even bring DEATH to your soul or your body. FIGHT FOR YOUR MIND! What could have been (fantasy or potential) and what is are totally different. Believe that you will make it!

2. Talk about it (in the beginning stages only) and get it all out! But beware: be careful who you put in this circle of trust. Not everyone who gives counsel gives wise advice or even has common sense. Before opening up to anyone it is important to ask yourself, "Is their walk in the Lord?"

3. Once you have let it all out, grieved, and are in the final stretch, STOP talking about it! Do not be deceived into thinking that talking about it over and over makes it better. That may be true in the beginning, but not toward the end. It actually causes you to prolong your complete healing. It brings the past into existence and delays the new that is still to come. When one door closes, rest assured that another one will open!

4. Do not overthink or dwell on your past relationship any longer! The mind does its building solely by the power of thought; so don't dwell! When the temptation comes to do so, hold the thought captive and reject it in Jesus's name! Do not entertain it and make this process a habit.

5. Don't try to find out how that person is doing through relatives, friends, or social media. What you don't feed will eventually

die! Move forward beyond your present leftover pain. Where you are and where you're going matters much more than where you've been.

6. Have a private funeral with a piece of paper with your ex's name written on it or something of theirs. They are not going to be in your future! Crumble it up as if the situation is pointless and bury it, because it's now a dead issue. Maybe burn it or flush it down the toilet or simply throw it in the garbage—whatever approach works for you. It is history, it is over, and it is finished!

7. Move forward with the mind-set that the relationship will never come to fruition rather than a "well, maybe it could have" mentality that only serves to keep useless hope alive. God never gives back what He takes away! If it was His perfect will, you would be together now. Nothing slips from His hands. Make sure you learn your lesson and don't repeat your mistake over and over again. There is a reason to everything that has happened, and this can lead to a testimony that can help others later.

8. Get rid of all lingering pictures or items of your relationship, even harmless-looking objects that somehow keep you in the past with this person with whom you no longer share a future. If you have children with them, perhaps keep some items for the sake of the child, but let a grandparent or a relative hold them. Your "new" will have greater value than your "old!"

9. Don't beat yourself up! You WILL be healed; day by day, not in a day. "Pastor Hery, when?" The answer is, whenever God believes you are ready! Be patient in your journey to recovery.

10. Don't compare the new that's coming with the old. Don't compare exceptions with the standard. Don't compare a Christian life as a child of God with a non-Christian life as a creation of God. Don't compare a child of God with a chosen child of God called for ministry, from whom God expects more. We don't really know what's happening out there anyway, as there are many actors and factors. What worked for a couple of non-Christians may not work for you as His child. God will not be outdone, as He desires to give you His best!

In summary, it's easy to go back to old familiar ghosts if we become lazy and passive in our thinking. It takes courage not to look back, and you have it because Christ Himself says that we are more than conquerors! You are not just a regular conqueror but "more than" one. It's very rewarding to look into a blank future knowing through faith that it will be filled with God's promises. Believe that there is a "next thing" coming in your life. Make the "next thing" the "best thing" by learning from the "last thing."

Don't confuse just getting by with overcoming. Don't confuse coping with healing! Coping covers the pain; healing deals with the pain, accepts the truth, and makes better choices. Running from a problem or an issue does not make it go away. Face it, so you can conquer it! The truth sets you free, but it also can make you miserable until you face it! Do not pretend anymore, as we all have issues or problems once in a while.

Understand once and for all that you must cast down those thoughts of yesterday and go toward the new possibilities that await you. This, however, will require effort and determination. The good news is that God will do His part when you do yours. Therefore, go ahead right now and cut the cords that keep you tied up and stagnant! Your Light has come to show you the things that are before you. Walk by faith and not by past memories. Make a decision to buckle up in this emotional, bumpy ride so you can endure, resist, and heal. Turn your life from "EX" to Excellence, and heal in the mighty name of Jesus!

7

COMMITTED TO LOVING RIGHT

Therefore a man shall leave his father and mother and
be joined to his wife, and they shall become one flesh.

—Genesis 2:24

HERE IS NO one on this planet with whom you
can become one other than your spouse. Your
children are a blessing from the Lord, but they are
a temporary assignment, as they will leave and form their
own lives. Your parents are also a blessing, but at some
point, we have to cut that umbilical cord. Your spouse, on
the other hand, is with whom God has united you to be
one. You are twice as powerful together. As it is written
in Ecclesiastes 4:12, "Though one may be overpowered by
another, two can withstand him. And a threefold cord is
not quickly broken." God's purpose in marriage is to unite
a man and a woman according to His divine destiny for
His kingdom glory.

This chapter will primarily focus on married couples,
because a "dragged out and enduring" marriage can
really be a challenge to being ALL IN for God. Marriage
was designed to be enjoyable and fruitful with the
union growing in love. In His Word, God speaks of

love 697 different times, so it's safe to believe that love is the cornerstone from which all things start. If you don't understand love, then you really can't understand marriage. Couples who live on purpose, growing in love and chasing together after the presence of a mighty God, are drawn closer by His love. Unfortunately, some today are married and begin their Christ-walk already behind the eight ball. It will require a lot of prayer, fasting, and a bulldog-tenacious and committed mind-set to trust in the Great I Am to bring restoration. One thing I can surely encourage you with today—God is able!

Speaking of commitment, allow me to emphasize that there is a difference between interest and commitment. When you're interested in doing something, you do it only when it's convenient. When you're committed to something, you accept no excuses, only results. When a person doesn't want to commit, they are avoiding the Cross, because commitment means to die to yourself and live the way God commands. Those who reject the Cross are enemies of the Cross. The best God-centered marriages are those where two people are best friends, excellent at forgiving, and committed to each other.

There are only two options regarding commitment: you're either in or you're out. A wishy-washy commitment can go either way and will definitely not stand life's fiery trials. Commitment demands a choice, but "could be" will usually preface it. You must know that until you're committed, you can't win. I wonder what would happen if, in the "whatever" moment of your life you're in today, you threw your whole self into it. When we throw our whole self (soul, spirit, and body) into committing wholeheartedly to our marriage and to putting our trust in God, He is able to do exceedingly abundantly. Sometimes we as humans want to help God so much, but the thing He asks of us the most is to trust Him. Keep praying, keep believing, and keep trusting in the Great I Am.

It's important to understand that if you deny yourself commitment, the options you have for your life will be sorely limited. Everything in life that we truly desire requires an ALL IN, committed mind-set. Commitment creates a level of hope and trust when life's challenges come our way. Men, if you have issues with commitment like I've had, learn to love and listen better. Position yourself to flourish in life with your wife. It is your responsibility to step out of your shell, release your fears, and give a deeper meaning to your life by giving value to your relationships, especially the one with your wife, by choosing to love her just as Christ loved the church.

Commitment goes more smoothly when the roles are well defined and the couple commits to their covenant marriage. Married couples that serve each other and can unite forces for various churches or ministries, or simply serve together on purpose in their respective ministries, are a solid structure for our society and to the kingdom of heaven.

By the way, commitments don't have anything to do with your feelings. You commit to winning souls, loving your neighbor, and loving your spouse because it is the right thing to do. Stop expecting to be rewarded for what you're supposed to do. Stop bragging about how you do this for them or how much you love them—you're supposed to be doing that. I'm not impressed with people who talk big but are not committed. Commitment is the bridge between what you know and what you do! Stop allowing past hurts, fear, perfectionism, self-doubt, or your desire for independence to sabotage the future God has in store for you. Stop being so passive and RiseUp to embrace all that God wants for you.

Four Foundational Marriage Tips

I wanted to provide four tips here that will help this commitment stay alive and vibrant. However, keep in mind that it will require work, as nothing truly worthwhile is easy to achieve.

1. SHARE EVERYTHING

This means no secrets, because whatever you withhold will eventually bring resentment. I'm talking about a mutual dedication to transparency where both spouses are ALL IN; where you are naked and unashamed for each other; where you each have access to the other's phone, checkbook, and social media passwords.

2. PRIORITIZE YOUR SPOUSE OVER EVERYTHING ELSE EXCEPT GOD AND HEALTH

We don't need to live the single lifestyle anymore once we are married. Your thoughts and concerns need to be about your mate, not just yourself. Furthermore, do not complain in public about your spouse and their shortcomings. There are probably a lot of single folks that would love to take them off your hands! Give your mate the attention that he or she needs and be grateful of the person with whom God has allowed you to share life.

3. TAKE A VACATION EVERY THREE MONTHS

Water and relationships turn stale when not allowed to flow. Routines are a necessary part of life, but so should be spontaneous outings that bring a refreshing spark to any union.

4. Go out on a DATE (continued courting) once a week

Regardless of the fact that you may have small children at home, "couple time" is mandatory. The main relationship in your life should be between you and your spouse. A date doesn't need to be a long or expensive affair. It can be a quiet hour just having coffee together, enjoying dinner by yourselves, or catching a movie and taking a walk afterward to discuss it—something that will place you in a setting where you can talk, rekindle, and stay connected outside of your normal whirlwind routine.

Principles to Improve Your Marriage

Lastly, I would like to share some important principles I have come up with as well as some sound wisdom that our marriage counselor, Apostle Duane Swilley, shared with my wife and me before we got married. Any paraphrasing of Rev. Swilley's guidelines is only to make them as crystal clear as possible and to make them fit herein. I truly believe that any marriage can succeed if the couple has the right guidance and a true and mutual desire on the part of the husband and wife. I pray these twelve principles will help your marriage blossom.

1. Men—if you want her to submit, you will have to lay down your life for her

Women desire to feel safe and secure along with unconditional love. If a woman feels unstable or insecure in the commitment or love, she won't blossom to her fullest capability of being the ideal helpmate for her husband.

2. WOMEN—YOU SET THE ATMOSPHERIC THERMOSTAT IN YOUR HOME

Men desire to come home to a peaceful setting. Their home is their haven. If a man comes home to a combative and argumentative wife, expect him to stay at work longer or look for excuses to stay away. The Bible says the desires of a wife's heart will be to her husband. If a wife has "bad desires" in her heart for her husband, this ill feeling will reel around on her and indirectly affect her and the family.

3. ALL CAN BE COMPROMISED EXCEPT GOD, SO BE FLEXIBLE

The more flexible and agreeable we are with God, the less we need to be broken. The same applies with our spouse. The stronger person in a real relationship usually changes first! "Blessed are the flexible, for they shall not get bent out of shape, they shall chill some and they won't live so stringently"—Heriberto 3:16. Of course, I'm joking here. I certainly hope no one went to their Bible to look that up!

But seriously, flexibility is a gift that will help you not get so bent out of shape. Very few people have the ability to adapt on the fly and make quick adjustments that work unless they practice. We must accept the fact that everything doesn't always have to go according to plan. In fact, when you insist on things always going according to plan, you become stagnant and mechanical and lose that natural ability to adjust when plans suddenly change due to unexpected circumstances.

Yes, you can reschedule that meeting or outing, you can change your mind to regroup later, you can deviate from your "planned sex" at 11:10 p.m. when the news is over, and you can learn to better go with the flow. You have to be willing to fail if you're going to trust yourself to act from the gut and then adapt as you go. Keep changing, keep growing, and stay moldable—as individuals and as a couple. What the Bible promises as "two shall become one" is not an overnight transformation.

4. BEING RIGHT DOESN'T GIVE YOU PERMISSION TO BE DISRESPECTFUL

Most men don't just want hips and lips, but a piece of heaven at home in the midst of life's storms. A wise woman develops her inner beauty, seeks wisdom, and learns how to respect and speak to her husband with kindness. A husband has to consider what is written in 1 Peter 3:7: "Husbands, likewise, dwell with them with understanding, giving honor to the wife, as to the weaker vessel, and as being heirs together of the grace of life, that your prayers may not be hindered." There is no excuse for you to be constantly rude to your spouse—or anybody else, for that matter.

Rudeness is the weak person's imitation of strength. Little people belittle people just as hurt people hurt people! Be one that encourages and lifts up people instead of looking for the worst in others. Being nasty or mean-spirited is not a Christlike characteristic. Likewise, if you are the recipient of a rude person's constant barrage of jabs, insults, and barbs, let them know in a non-antagonistic way that you don't appreciate their treatment or attitude. If they continue, you must come to understand that the less you respond back to rude, critical, or argumentative people, the more peaceful your life will become.

5. DON'T STOP DATING OR LOOKING GOOD JUST BECAUSE YOU'RE MARRIED

Ladies, as if you didn't already know, men are visual creatures. The bedroom is not the place to wear your Winnie the Pooh or Betty Boop pajamas. Just because the car has been bought (marriage), it does not mean you should now take your foot off the pedal. Put those ratty and tacky outfits in a shoe box and donate them to him as rags for car washing. Of course I'm being comical here, but I think you get the picture.

Men, just because you've courted her and won her over, it does not mean you now can stay at home every weekend. It is vital to your marriage that you both continue doing the things that caused your love to flourish. Love never forgets the little things. A successful and godly marriage is all about growing in love with the same person over and over again! Remember the goal isn't getting married; the goal is *staying* married.

6. THERE IS ABSOLUTELY NO EXCUSE TO END UP IN ANOTHER PERSON'S BEDROOM

Temptation is real, and most of us will be tempted to be unfaithful at some point in our marriage. We must make a covenant with God to be true and faithful because, after all, He is the one with whom we must first and foremost be faithful. Never stop flirting with your spouse and never start flirting with anyone else. People cheat for unmet needs. If you have an unmet need in your marriage, express that need to your spouse. Don't go outside the marriage to have it met. Don't bring someone else along on a journey that is intended to be for only two—marriage is between two, and only two, people. Cheating is a choice that a person makes; it is not something forced upon us. It is an elective choice, not an accident or a mistake. RiseUp and wise up! Understand that betrayal happens when you give someone who doesn't deserve it too much access over your life.

7. LET LOVE CONTINUE TO FLOW BY PRAYING AND GOING TO CHURCH TOGETHER

It is vital to maintain the "right image" for your spouse. I know for a fact that if you work on spiritual intimacy, physical intimacy will improve. Understand that a prayer life is absolutely essential to a marriage. God will help you connect in ways that you can't connect by yourself. Statistics prove that couples that pray and go to church together have a better chance of avoiding divorce.

8. SETTLE ALL ISSUES EVERY DAY AND BEFORE BEDTIME

My friend and premarital marriage counselor, Apostle Duane Swilley, suggests that we should to do a "baggage check" before passing through the front door after a day's work. I personally like to have thirty minutes to an hour of just quiet time before we tackle the issues and pending responsibilities of life.

One of the sixteen covenants my wife and I made is to never go to bed angry. The Bible agrees with that bit of wisdom, as we read in Ephesians 4:26: "Be angry, and do not sin; do not let the sun go down on your wrath." The best marriages consist of two outstanding givers and forgivers. I don't care how mad you are or how unsettled your feelings are—you kiss your spouse good-night. Don't let the pending issue magnify itself any further. It doesn't need to be a passionate kiss, it can just be a peck—but do so, because tomorrow is new day.

9. DON'T LET ANYONE SPEAK ILL OF YOUR SPOUSE OR TEAR APART YOUR COVENANT

You chose to marry your spouse, which reflects on your decision-making ability. Take the initiative to stop gossip or slander when it pertains to your spouse. Satan has power, but he doesn't have authority. Protect your covenant union at all times.

10. IF AN ARGUMENT DRAGS ON WAY TOO LONG, BE THE MATURE ONE AND STRIP NAKED

I know some of you are probably cracking up right now, but that's exactly what this approach does. Laughter defuses tension. Long, drawn-out arguments don't resolve anything, but talking about things does help. Be wise enough to get over arguments, debates, fights, and quarrels quickly!

11. THE PAST IS OFF LIMITS

When couples rehash the past, it unnecessary rips off the scabs of past wounds. Your former partner represents your past. There is a reason they are in your past. It certainly is not for you to compare them to your present spouse or bring them up unnecessarily. If a fight occurred months ago, let it stay in the past; today is a new day. That earlier issue is history and does not pertain to any present issues. Don't bring it up! If your destiny was in Egypt, the Red Sea would have never closed! Stop pressing replay on the things or people that need to be deleted from your life. Understand that the life in front of you is far more important than the life behind you.

12. LEARN TO STUDY YOUR SPOUSE AND TRY TO CHANGE PLACES WITH THEM (SEE THINGS FROM THEIR PERSPECTIVE)

When a spouse pauses to see the angle or perspective of their mate, it usually allows them to better understand that person. You need to be a student of your spouse. I know couples that gel together so well that one finishes the other's sentence while the other is still speaking.

In conclusion, getting married is awesome, but staying married is the bomb. Married couples, please do whatever you need to do to make your union work. Sometimes the roller coaster will be going up, sometimes it will be headed down, but God wants you to rely on Him throughout the entire ride. Growing marriages aren't determined by how much you have in common, but by how graciously you deal with your differences. Forgiveness is an expression of love, so choose to forgive quickly. It's a choice to show mercy. Those that show mercy have a sweeter and more delightful marriage. When mercy is absent, the marriage struggles and setbacks surface. I'm convinced that if two people make it their goal to imitate the humility of Christ, everything else will take care of itself.

One last point: keep in mind that marriage is not a 50–50 proposition but divorce certainly is. Marriage has to be a 100–100 endeavor on the part of both parties. It isn't about dividing everything in half but about giving everything you've got. You never lose by loving, but you always lose by holding back. Therefore, be ALL IN for your spouse and enjoy the closest relationship on earth, like Christ's great love for His church.[1]

life. Understand that the life in front of you is far more important than the life behind you.

12. LEARN TO STUDY YOUR SPOUSE AND TRY TO CHANGE PLACES WITH THEM (SEE THINGS FROM THEIR PERSPECTIVE)

When a spouse pauses to see the angle or perspective of their mate, it usually allows them to better understand that person. You need to be a student of your spouse. I know couples that get together so well that one finishes the other's sentence while the other is still speaking.

In conclusion, getting married is awesome, but staying married is the bomb. Married couples, please do whatever you need to do to make your union work. Sometimes the roller coaster will be going up, sometimes it will be headed down, but God wants you to rely on Him throughout the entire ride. Growing marriages aren't determined by how much you have in common, but by how graciously you deal with your differences. Forgiveness is an expression of love, so choose to forgive quickly. It's a choice to show mercy. Those that show mercy have a sweeter and more delightful marriage. When mercy is absent, the marriage struggles and setbacks surface. I'm convinced that if two people make it their goal to imitate the humility of Christ, everything else will take care of itself.

One last point: keep in mind that marriage is not a 50-50 proposition but divorce certainly is. Marriage has to be a 100-100 endeavor on the part of both parties. It isn't about dividing everything in half but about giving every thing you've got. You never lose by loving, but you always lose by holding back. Therefore, be ALL IN for your spouse and enjoy the closest relationship on earth, like Christ's great love for His church.

8

TEEN PARENTING WISDOM

Through wisdom a house is built, and
by understanding it is established.

—Proverbs 24:3

THE LONGER I live, the more I realize the value and
influence of parents. Your children will keep you on
your knees, but that is not such a bad thing. It will
help you stay humble and dependent on the almighty God.
It's a place of proper perspective where we receive insight
and discernment from our heavenly Father. Children
need to be trained early on like wet cement (when both
are still malleable) because when they grow into teenagers,
the teachings many times fall on deaf ears. At that stage,
rebellion and stubbornness rise up when correction is
given because the child has become too set in his or her
ways. As a matter of fact, at thirteen years of age a child is
pretty much already shaped spiritually.

Parents, please understand that it is easier to build strong
children than to repair broken ones. Correction must begin
in the home and be done with love, repetition (the key to
mastery), teaching, and denials when necessary, because
boundaries are instrumental to a child's development.

These boundaries will help them love themselves and become valuable members of society. I've heard many regrets from parents because they spoiled their children rather than disciplining them at an early age.

Deuteronomy 6:6–7 says, "These commandments that I give you today are to be on your hearts. Impress them on your children. Talk about them when you sit at home and when you walk along the road, when you lie down and when you get up" (NIV). Notice it says "impress" (like eyeglasses imprint on a nose) God's Word upon your children. Parents worry too much about their children's reactions toward the Bible rather than just doing what they are supposed to do: impress or share it.

Parents, please let me encourage you to simply plant the seed of truth and trust God to nourish it. Share, share, share and don't be too concerned if they don't have questions or comments; simply share the Word and pray for them (and not only on Sundays!). "Knee" your children into the kingdom of God. Believe with all you've got that God's Word (indeed, His promise) and your discipline will bring forth a fruitful harvest in your child's life. Keep Jesus attractive and reachable for them as you spend quality time with them in the Word and in family fun. Parents, please don't forget that life happens at the speed of light, whether or not we're paying attention!

So your son or daughter is now a teenager; now what? You as a parent did some things right and some things wrong as he grew up. She is now almost an adult, and perhaps conversations don't go quite as smoothly as before. Allow me to take some pressure off of you right now by saying that no parent is perfect and neither are the children they raise. You can alleviate the awkwardness of this stage by always being real and transparent with them, telling them your mistakes and encouraging them not to make the same mistakes.

If you are raising a teenager on your own as a single parent, you are fully aware that correcting or disciplining them at this stage is much more challenging. If it isn't, then stick around a little longer! Besides surrendering them to the Lord, the next most important task to take on is to change hats from a disciplinarian to a counselor, so to speak. I'm not suggesting you allow them to now run the house, but you need to pray for wisdom for all of your disciplinary undertakings. During this stage, you go from rescuing them all the time to allowing the teen to occasionally fail by stepping back. If they learn to handle failures with the smaller things, they eventually will be able to handle failure and disappointments with larger issues. Teaching your child how to handle and deal with failure makes them more responsible. We are not here to pick up the broken pieces but to help, advise, and counsel our kids and hopefully keep things from breaking in the first place. Make sure that in this process you listen to them and allow them to express themselves freely and without judgment in order to keep the channels of communication open. Do not bully them around. When you cannot or will not relate to your teenager, Satan and his demons will!

Parents, what you say and do will affect your children. Do more than dictate and yell; be an example of love, joy, forgiveness, and peace. Every teen is different; some need more attention than others, but all need a mother's love and a fatherly example. If you are alone and the child's other parent is missing, just do your very best and pray for God to bridge the gap. Parents, the bottom line is that there are no guarantees; however, if you really want to maximize your connection with your teenager, make sure you accept their uniqueness, affirm their value, trust them with responsibility, help them build their own character, support their dreams or potential, correct them without condemning them (keep in mind to praise in public and criticize in private), and, of course, love them unconditionally.

We know that discipline is crucial, but the wrong kind of discipline can lead to rebellion and resentment. When discipline is done with humiliation (ridicule), anger, comparison, bribery, abusive criticism, antipathy, or with the expectation of perfection, it will create a negative atmosphere which will lead only to strife and hostility. Make sure you stay in control; you are the adult, after all. Be their encourager! Also understand that not everything your child does requires your attention, so don't be a nag. The Word says in Colossians 3:21, "Fathers, do not provoke your children, lest they become discouraged." This means you should give them some space. It's discipline without exasperation.

Fathers, make a decision to be ALL IN for Christ so you can be the spiritual paragon in your family. Satan desires to kill the family, and that destruction starts with the head. God ordained that the priests of Israel speak blessings in His name over their own children. It is much more important for your children to be well grounded than well rounded. Be the example. Live what you preach. Focus more on preparing your kids for eternity than for college.

Here are twelve tips to help you become a better parent to your teenager:

Teenage Parenting Tips

1. Do not take things personally or become defensive. Put your feelings aside even if it hurts.

2. Love your children continuously and unconditionally right where they are, no matter what.

3. Be patient and respectful of their transition from a child to an adult. One of the main reasons teens need strong, wise, mentoring, loving parents is because without them, many will spend most of their lives trying to figure out exactly who they are.

4. Accept the fact they are not a child anymore—give them some rope. If a teen feels she is mature enough to rebel, then she needs to be responsible enough to care for herself.

5. Pray, pray, pray for their future, blessing them with declared words. Never give up on your children, just as our heavenly Father never gives up on us.

6. Choose your battles wisely; arguments aggravate and incite their present rebellious state. Every parent should remember that one day their teen will follow their example more than their advice.

7. Limit or reduce your lectures. Sometimes it's more important to listen to them and their opinions without giving correction.

8. Show and tell them that you love them, that you're there for them when they need you. Understand that when purpose is lacking and boredom is rampant, many teenagers start experimenting with gangs, sex, alcohol, and drugs to help cope with their void,

insecurities, and anxieties. They are too inexperienced to see these things are all false escapes.

As a parent, it's so difficult to see the pain and suffering in a child who is caught up in addiction knowing that there is nothing you can do except pray and be there for them. You want to wipe away their tears and take it all away—that's love. Our Abba Father wants to wipe away our tears and take our pain away too; that is why He sent His Son to take on our pain and burden. Call on Him because He is near and He is waiting. While I myself believe in miracles, I also know that ultimately the choice to become free of addiction can only be made by your child. Pray that God's Spirit touches their soul.

Parents, teach your children to follow a dream by allowing them to explore and venture out. Encourage them to develop healthy habits like exercising and practicing good nutrition to develop a fit body. Hearten them to pursue a career by enrolling in college, vocational school, or the military. All of these are important, but most of all, keep taking them to church so that the Word of God is impressed upon them until their purpose is revealed or maturity sets in. We as parents are to train our children in the ways of the Lord from the time they are toddlers so that as they grow to become teenagers or adults, they are aware of the ways of the Lord until their last day on earth. Enrolling them in a church youth program is vitally important because it provides a sense of belonging while they deal with their insecurities, questions, and rebellion. Many times they will "leave the things of God to taste the world" only to return because of what you or the church impressed upon them at an early age.

We don't wait until our kids are fifteen or sixteen to let them choose if they want to go to school, right? No way! Well, we need to apply the same principle when it comes to teaching our kids about our Lord Jesus Christ. The world's thinking is twisted; I've heard many parents say, "I won't force my faith or religion on my children. When they get older, they can choose for themselves if they want to learn about God." Nonsense! This deceptive "open minded" mentality is destructive to your children's future. The Bible says in Joshua 24:15, "And if it seems evil to you to serve the LORD, choose for yourselves this day whom you will serve, whether the gods which your fathers served that were on the other side of the River, or the gods of the Amorites, in whose land you dwell. But as for me and my house, we will serve the LORD." Let this verse be an anchor to your family by choosing God today and being ALL IN for Him, His will, and His plan!

9. Express feelings carefully and with tact, because a soft answer turns away wrath. The Book of Proverbs says, "A soft answer turns away wrath, but a harsh word stirs up anger" (Prov. 15:1). Talk to your children without

snooping (unless the danger of drugs or
other deadly influence is present), and offer
advice. Make it a point to spend quality
time with them.

10. Show compassion even if they are
unappreciative or ungrateful and don't get
where you're coming from.

11. Live with faith and expect a miracle;
God will never dismiss the prayers of a
loving parent.

12. Stop blaming yourself and adding guilt
to your life because you weren't a perfect
parent. News flash: there are no perfect
parents other than our heavenly Father.
Don't be too hard on yourself when your
children fail to follow your example. Not
everyone who once followed Jesus remained
with Him. Parents are responsible for setting
examples and children are responsible for
following them, so be sure to check your
example before you check your children. The
real failure in parenting is the parent who's
not around to be a good example.

PART 3

THE POWER OF A MADE-UP MIND

9

DEFEATING DOUBLE-MINDEDNESS

But let him ask in faith, with no doubting, for he
who doubts is like a wave of the sea driven and
tossed by the wind. For let not that man suppose
that he will receive anything from the Lord; he is
a double-minded man, unstable in all his ways.

—JAMES 1:6–8

MOST OF US occasionally battle double-mindedness regarding our faith. We are ambivalent, fickle, or erratic concerning our relationship with God. Don't beat yourself up, but don't stay stuck in that unsure and undependable thinking either. There is so much information available to us, so many sources of wisdom—books, preachers, teachers—that it is easy to become uncertain about what is right and what is a well-meaning absolute truth or even deception. A double-minded person is driven by too many opinions and by intimidation. The problem is that this wavering or vacillating results in us receiving nothing from the Lord, because you can't walk with God holding hands with the devil—otherwise known as serving two masters—for our God is a jealous God.

Every day we face conflict between the easy way and the right way. Many people spend their lives regretting their past and fearing their future while missing out on the moment. You cannot build a powerful present living that way. Therefore, we need to embark in the mission of renewing our minds and getting filled with Jesus so that we can refocus and get our lives back. We have to ask God for wisdom and allow Him to break us so that we operate under His perfect will and a made-up mind. The heart that is broken before the Lord is opened not only to allow all the infection out but also to allow the healing and purification cleansing in. God wants to know where you stand in your heart with your relationship with Him. Matthew 12:30 says, "He who is not with Me is against Me, and he who does not gather with Me scatters abroad."

Sin is a spiritual issue, not a moral issue; a separation from God's will and His purpose. The righteous live content, but the ungodly are never satisfied. There is always a back-and-forth conflict within. The Book of Habakkuk says, "See, the enemy is puffed up; his desires are not upright—but the righteous person will live by his faithfulness—indeed, wine betrays him; he is arrogant and *never* at rest. Because he is as greedy as the grave and like death is *never satisfied*" (2:4–5, NIV, emphasis added).

Double-minded people have a destabilizing need to change; they waver and are indecisive. They live with doubt, are inconsistent, and easily get frustrated. They have an inability to move forward, and they live in a confused state of mind. Their word is worthless. Moreover, they are never satisfied or content because they have allowed two different mind-sets to coexist. They have not made Jesus their Lord and master, and despite the very real fact that they want some of Jesus, they continue to be shackled to the very chains that bind them. Quite exhausting, if you ask me! Revelation 3:15–16 says, "I know your works: you are neither cold nor hot. Would that you were either cold or hot! So, because you are lukewarm, and neither hot nor cold, I will spit you out of my mouth" (ESV).

Let me just lay it out there as straightforward as I can: life is less difficult when you make up your mind to die to self! By dying to self, you acknowledge that you are giving up your "vote" and yielding your will to live surrendered to His will (lordship).

If you want to gain spiritual truth, to know God more personally, to have the Holy Spirit fill your life completely, to understand the Bible more, to receive more answers to your prayers, to see more people get saved, and to personally lead more people to Christ, then yield to God completely. You can accomplish this by doing His will, guarding your mind and heart, and resisting the enemy. God will give you more spiritual truth and reveal Himself to you more intimately. He will give you more understanding of the Scriptures, answer more of your prayers, and place people who need to be saved in your path. However, as long as you continue to dabble in deliberate sin and bow to Him only on Sundays, you will be unsteady and unbalanced in all your ways and these blessings will be thwarted. You can't be heavenly minded and worldly minded at the same time and expect supernatural, heaven-sent blessings to enter your life. You have to live with a made-up mind to grow spiritually. Understand that physical maturity is bound to time, but spiritual maturity is bound to obedience. Choose today who will be the master of your soul.

CHARACTERISTICS OF A DOUBLE-MINDED PERSON

First of all, chill out and keep in mind that from time to time we all exhibit some or all of the traits that characterize a double-minded person. Therefore, as Psalm 37 in the King James Bible tells us, "Fret not thyself" (v. 1). Be aware, but don't dwell on them nor let them weigh down your soul.

A double-minded person does the following:

1. PRAYS, BUT DOUBTS

2. HEARS THE WORD, BUT DOES NOT ACT UPON IT

> But be doers of the word, and not hearers only, deceiving yourselves. For if anyone is a hearer of the word and not a doer, he is like a man who looks intently at his natural face in a mirror. For he looks at himself and goes away and at once forgets what he was like. But the one who looks into the perfect law, the law of liberty, and perseveres, being no hearer who forgets but a doer who acts, he will be blessed in his doing.
>
> —JAMES 1:22–25, ESV

The Bible references the carnal Christian, that is, someone who makes decisions with his or her natural senses, whereas the spiritual Christian is a believer who makes decisions by walking in the Spirit's leading. For example, the carnal Christian may hear a prophetic word and then wonder if it is true! Living this way fills your life with double-mindedness. We can't be professing the things of Christ and then acting like sinners, asking God for things that feed the flesh rather than asking for His will to be done.

3. SPEAKS GOOD THINGS, BUT ALSO SPEAKS BAD THINGS

> From the same mouth come blessing and cursing. My brothers, these things ought not to

be so. Does a spring pour forth from the same
opening both fresh and salt water? Can a fig tree,
my brothers, bear olives, or a grapevine produce
figs? Neither can a salt pond yield fresh water.

—JAMES 3:10–12, ESV

The double-minded Israelites were repeatedly thrown
back into the wilderness because they couldn't stay
committed. Live what you believe. Refreshing and
cleansing freshwater cannot come from a saltwater source.
Make the right choice and stay committed to it. There is
power in our words, the ability to create the life you seek.
Therefore, speak things that build and edify. Create your
destiny—speak life!

4. LOVES, BUT ALSO HATES

Anyone who claims to be in the light but hates a
brother or sister is still in the darkness.

—1 JOHN 2:9, NIV

5. LOVES WITH WORDS, BUT NOT WITH DEEDS

Dear children, let us not love with words or
speech but with actions and in truth.

—1 JOHN 3:18, NIV

6. PROMISES WITH THEIR WORD, BUT DOES NOT HONOR IT

Let what you say be simply "Yes" or "No"; anything
more than this comes from evil.

—MATTHEW 5:37, ESV

This is my biggest pet peeve. I can't trust or depend on
a person who doesn't honor their word. Unfortunately, the

great majority of people don't. Integrity is something that is sorely lacking in our society. Don't get caught up in this racket. I realize that a person's actions may show you what their words perhaps cannot; however, I firmly believe that a person rises or falls to the level of their confession and word. Contrary to popular belief, what you think and say matters as much as what you do.

7. TRUSTS GOD, BUT ONLY TO A DEGREE, RELYING ON OVER-ANALYSIS AND REASONING

> Cursed is the man who trusts in man and makes flesh his strength, whose heart departs from the LORD.
>
> —JEREMIAH 17:5

Turmoil sets in when we try to put self into the supernatural. King Saul was double-minded. He also was probably psychotic, demonstrated by his practice of consulting witches and at times even asking David to calm his demonic spirit. His capriciousness, which led him to try to intervene in God's plans, went as far as planning to kill David. But God knows all our plans, and He knew Saul's. He directed David to sneak into Saul's bedroom and cut a piece of Saul's clothing while he slept, basically giving Saul the message, "Hey dude, I was so close to you that I could've killed you, and you had no clue!" Saul perceived this and quickly changed his mind about killing David, yet his double-mindedness was so strong that he changed it back and moved forward with his quest to kill David yet again.

8. ASSOCIATES WITH POSITIVE PEOPLE WHO BUILD, BUT ALSO KEEPS THE NEGATIVE ONES

> Do not be deceived: "Evil company corrupts good habits."
>
> —1 Corinthians 15:33

Sometimes we have to rid ourselves of certain people—toxic people—because when we get rid of wrong people, bad things stop happening for the most part. However, when the right people enter our lives, it only builds us and takes us closer to our destiny and ultimate potential. When Peter allowed Jesus into his life, fish began jumping into his boat. However, when a Jonah gets on your boat, it can start to sink. Once the sailors threw Jonah overboard, the storm suddenly subsided!

Some people make your "boat" prosper, and others, unfortunately, can cause it to sink. Ask God for discernment and wisdom on whom to keep and whom to keep at a distance. Separating yourself like this may sting a little, but we must understand that although failures will happen, repeated failures may be the result of allowing the wrong people to get too close. We need to do more than just associate with positive people who build us up; we also need to rid our lives of the negative ones who destroy and cause us to stay in the wilderness or in bondage living.

Defeating Double-Mindedness

There is no prescription to cure double-mindedness; it requires a choice of the will. Following are a few ways we can make the right choice and gradually change for good:

1. Draw nearer to God

> Come near to God and he will come near to you. Wash your hands, you sinners, and purify your hearts, you double-minded.
>
> —James 4:8, niv

We have to get hungry and thirsty for God's righteousness (good standing). I don't care how delicious the dish, you simply cannot feed people who are not hungry. When you want something, you've got to hunger and go for it!

2. CHANGE YOUR HEART BY RENEWING YOUR MIND

> And do not be conformed to this world, but be transformed by the renewing of your mind, that you may prove what is that good and acceptable and perfect will of God.
>
> —ROMANS 12:2

3. CHANGE YOUR WAYS BY GETTING INTO HIS WORD

> Your word is a lamp to my feet and a light to my path.
>
> —PSALM 119:105

Many Christians go to the Bible as the last resort when they are seeking direction, preferring to discuss things with friends or their pastor (which is fine, but not 100 percent). You will learn a lot about God at church and through Christian fellowship, but you will come to know Him through spending time in the Word.

4. BECOME STEADFAST (SINGLE-MINDED) BY PRESSING FORWARD

> Brothers and sisters, I do not consider myself yet to have taken hold of it. But one thing I do: Forgetting what is behind and straining toward what is ahead, I press on toward the goal to win the prize for which God has called me heavenward in Christ Jesus.
>
> —PHILIPPIANS 3:13–14, NIV

5. SET YOUR MIND AND KEEP IT SET

> Set your minds on things that are above, not on
> things that are on earth.
>
> —COLOSSIANS 3:2, ESV

Many people fail at getting their desired results because their minds are not truly made up. They are carrying baggage instead of making a mental dump. It's ridiculous not to change if that change leads to improvement. It's futile not to release the mental baggage holding you back. And it's unproductive to live with a mind that is wishy-washy. Make up your mind and keep it set regardless of the opposition or resistance that may come.

6. TRUST WITHOUT TRYING TO FIGURE IT OUT OR ENGAGE IN SELF-UNDERSTANDING

> Trust in the LORD forever, for the LORD, the
> LORD himself, is the Rock eternal.
>
> —ISAIAH 26:4, NIV

7. DON'T FEAR, BECAUSE THERE IS NO IRREVERSIBLE "BLOWING IT" IN GOD

> So do not fear, for I am with you; do not
> be dismayed, for I am your God. I will
> strengthen you and help you; I will uphold
> you with my righteous right hand.
>
> —ISAIAH 41:10, NIV

If you make a mistake, even a huge one, your life is not ruined! We have to understand and believe that our Creator is a God who brings restoration to things lost, stolen, or destroyed. Some of us have gone bankrupt, chosen a wrong career path, or married the wrong person (despite the Bible's warnings about becoming unequally yoked). God has the power to make even the most circuitous paths straight. Too many Christians waste their lives in indecision because of fear.

8. WALK IN THE SPIRIT, NOT THE FLESH

> Since we are living by the Spirit, let us follow the Spirit's leading in every part of our lives.
> —GALATIANS 5:25, NLT

The best "search engine" is found in 1 Corinthians 2:10:

> But God has revealed them to us through His Spirit. For the Spirit searches all things, yes, the deep things of God.

The Spirit is never wrong. This truth is so inherent that it boggles my mind to think that many people don't consult with Him first over anything else. Trying to be heavenly minded and worldly-minded at the same time brings mega-frustrations. Since you cannot serve two masters, it is prudent that you make up your mind and decide which way you are going to live. Many things are so obvious that they really don't require a decision. For example, you don't need to deliberate about whether or not to leave your wife for your younger secretary. That choice should be very apparent. God's commandments make certain things crystal clear. Learn to listen for and obey His prompting because it will never lead you to do something that goes against His Word.

Some choices are left to you. When you wake up in the morning, the choice of which pants to wear is all yours. You don't need to call the church, spend time in prayer, and begin to fast until you hear God's voice saying, "Wear the Calvin Kleins." And then there are other decisions that require consultation with the Spirit of God. If you sow into the flesh, of the flesh you shall reap—and that crop will usually yield corruption. If you sow into the Spirit, however, you shall reap everlasting life! It's a no-brainer, but unfortunately many of us indulge cheerfully in the flesh only to bawl like babies later as we struggle in vain to get out of our mess.

Husbands, your families are saying, "Lead us." Choose wisely! God will not allow you to straddle the proverbial fence and grow in His image simultaneously; you will have to decide what you're willing to purify and what you're willing to burn away with the chaff.

9. Expect trials, temptations, and tribulations; but do not PANIC

> I have told you these things, so that in me you may have peace. In this world you will have trouble. But take heart! I have overcome the world.
>
> —John 16:33, NIV

In other words, don't be surprised when life's difficulties arrive. They're coming; it's not a matter of if, but when. However, God has equipped you to be a victorious overcomer, so "fret not thyself."

10. Be PATIENT in the process without cursing your life with doubting WORDS

> Whoever guards his mouth preserves his life; he who opens wide his lips comes to ruin.
>
> —Proverbs 13:3, ESV

THREE ADDITIONAL SIMPLE
WAYS TO OVERCOME

TRIALS

From the hand of God come trials that serve to build us up, develop endurance, enlarge our faith, and mature us in our walk with Christ.

TRUST

The more I read God's Word and get closer to Him, the more I am convinced that there is one main issue facing the American believer today: trust. Our culture has developed such a dependence on intellect and self-reliance that we immediately jump to the conclusion that there is no one to trust but ourselves.

TRUTH

Remember the teaching of our Lord Jesus who said, "No one can serve two masters," "Trust in the Lord with all your heart," and, "There is no other God but one" (see Matthew 6:24, Proverbs 3:5–6, and Isaiah 45:5). The truth is that there is no truth but His truth and no God but Him.

Jesus's name removes and evicts any other kingdom from your life. Evict all that is dead in your life and bring it to life by the power given to you by the living King of kings. God doesn't want someone who is lukewarm or double-minded, walking without passion and settling for a life of passivity. To put it more bluntly, if your walk with Christ is not costing you something, then you're still swimming in the shallow side of the pool. Stop waiting for perfection to emerge before deciding to move forward. Stop being defensive and shying away from correction that will edify. Stop seeking the approval of people rather than seeking what God wants for you. And stop being so hesitant that life takes you neither here nor there.

Do you know what happens when you hesitate in doing something that God has told you to do? Your adversary makes the first move. The devil gets that jump on you. The prophet Elijah experienced this with God's people, as is mentioned in 1 Kings 18:21: "And Elijah came to all the people, and said, 'How long will you falter between two opinions [hesitate]? If the LORD is God, follow Him; but if Baal, follow him.'" In other words, make a decision and stop wavering. Be bold and courageous like Joshua when he said, "And if it seems evil to you to serve the LORD, choose for yourselves this day whom you will serve [stop hesitating], whether the gods which your fathers served that were on the other side of the River, or the gods of the Amorites, in whose land you dwell. But as for me and my house, we will serve the LORD" (see Joshua 24:15). Friend, if you want to live by faith and be ALL IN, hesitation is one of the most hazardous habits you could ever have, and it comes from being indecisive.

The Bible says a man who is double-minded is "unstable and restless in all his ways [in everything he thinks, feels, or decides]" (James 1:8, AMP). If you are double-minded, the decisions you make are half-hearted, split, and weak. You try to live by faith and protect your fear at the same time. You make faith statements like, "I believe God is going to heal me," but then your fear whispers, "But I wouldn't want to say I'm well just yet." You're so busy going back and forth between faith and fear that you can't make any progress at all. It's time to rise up, be ALL IN, and kick the habit of hesitation today! Make a solid decision to trust and act completely regardless of whatever consequence comes from trusting in the Word of God. Settle it once and for all! Resolve to never again entertain doubts that paralyze you. When doubt tries to infiltrate your thoughts (which it will, because you're only human), cast it out quickly. When God speaks, don't waste a second—step right out in faith. That way you can always keep the devil a step behind you! And do so with confidence, knowing that God's ways will never disappoint you.

Let me press a little deeper and give you three additional stumbling blocks that lead to double-mindedness. First, and my least favorite, is seeking perfectionism rather than excellence. I personally don't want perfection; I want effort. Life isn't about perfection, but progress! Therefore, stop trying to impress yourself with your attempts at perfection. Nobody has it 100 percent together. In fact, Ecclesiastes 7:20 says, "For there is not a just man on earth who does good and does not sin." Therefore, get started and do good with exactly what you have at hand now. It's better to do something imperfectly than to do nothing flawlessly. That's why I'm convinced that done is better than perfect!

The second obstacle that brings forth double-mindedness is a defensive mind-set toward correction or constructive criticism. Let's be real here for a moment—nobody really likes correction or criticism! I know I flinch somewhat when it's done to me. We love our comfort zone and would rather stay the same without needing correction. However, correction is necessary for our guidance, direction, and protection. Usually what we hate is often what we're called to correct. The Bible says in Proverbs 12:1, "Whoever loves discipline loves knowledge, but whoever hates correction is stupid" (NIV). I've observed that when you correct a double-minded person, two things happen: they feel rejected or they get rebellious. Hey, I know it's not fun, especially when it is unsolicited or done harshly. But whether it's bad timing, a wrong attitude, invited or not, let criticism force you to examine yourself.

Nobody has or ever will arrive at perfection, because we all have issues and areas in need of improvement. However, the fact of the matter is that we live in a super-sensitive society where people are too fragile to be corrected or too religious to be told anything. We want information but don't want instruction. A caveat before I continue: be careful who you allow to pour instruction or correction into your life. Their wisdom could be stifled. It is important to understand, though, that correction without a relationship will feel like abuse. This is why praise is vital before correction; it's like a vitamin to the soul. Therefore, stop being so quick to correct people. Correction is necessary, but make sure you have deposited love first.

It is important to realize that many are living in foolish rebellion, some are too stiff-necked (stubborn), and others are just too prideful to receive or embrace beneficial correction. Ask God for wisdom, and stop treating those who refuse the medicine! Just be silent, smile, and pray for them—which, by the way, is one of the most precious acts of love you can do. Disobedience to God's Word is costly enough (none will escape) without your added forced input. Most people will learn more through life's humbling lessons than from an out-of-control, correcting tongue that lashes out. Realize that when a person hardens his heart after being corrected, his behavior usually becomes erratic because a person will not change beyond the level of their submission. I'm convinced that learning to accept and give correction with love (and, of course, tact and the right tone of voice) is a major part of growth.

Still, many people continue to get defensive and quickly reject constructive correction or criticism. Now sometimes we may have to do that because not all correction and constructive criticism is valid, but we must be wise enough to listen anyway (especially when it comes from those people who really care about us), because if we don't, it can limit our mental, emotional, and spiritual growth.

Go further by asking God if He is trying to tell you something. Understand that medicine and criticism (correction) may not sit well at first, but they eventually bring the needed result. Even an enemy can be a blessing if you pray for them and not hate them, as is mentioned in Psalm 23:5: "You prepare a table before me in the presence of my enemies; You anoint my head with oil; my cup runs over." In fact, you may grow to a place of indebtedness to this person. You may one day feel the need to take them out to dinner or buy them a small gift since they drove you to pray harder, be more determined, and improve in an area that God was trying to remove from your life. Therefore, thank everyone who took the time to correct or criticize you with sincere intentions.

The last obstacle is the need to seek approval from people rather than from God. It doesn't matter how positive or polished you are, how many people you try to help, or even how many times you've read the book *How to Win Friends and Influence People*— you simply cannot please everyone. There will always be the proverbial "someone" who is not for you. You try figuring them out, but it just doesn't flow. It's all good…move on! It doesn't really matter anyway; celebrate life with those who celebrate you. Accept the fact that there will always be someone who, due to their unhappiness, cynicism, or because they are insecure in themselves, will feel the need to critique you. They will question, either in silence or vociferously, everything about you—even how you dot your i's and cross your t's. Keep moving forward doing what you were placed on this earth to do. Keep loving and helping people. But don't ever doubt yourself.

Many of us seek external validation when we should be focused on internal peace. Be free in the fact that you do not have to entertain those who doubt or don't understand you. It's fine to live a life others don't understand. I will accept God's Word and purpose for my life over the opinion of people every single time. Don't be distracted from your destiny by trying to manage people's opinions. While everyone is entitled to their opinion, not everyone is entitled to their own truth. Most won't understand your purpose anyway, so why bother putting so much value in what they think or say? You will never be able to please everyone, so you might as well make up your mind right now to do what God, not you or man, has purposed you to do. And keep in mind that truth usually offends those who are living a lie.

Therefore, don't change who you are; instead, improve upon your character, for there is always room for growth. There's no need to change so people will like you; be yourself and the right people will love the real you. Don't let the opinion of a few stop you from the many God has in store for you! Don't base your identity on other people's perceptions of you. Popularity doesn't validate you or define you; you're not validated by numbers anyway. I've been "different" all my life, and I didn't really start living until I stopped apologizing for being me. Remember first and foremost that you are fearfully and wonderfully made. Now be all that God (not people) wants you to be.

I've personally come to the realization that if you love yourself and have confidence in God, others will take note of it and they'll be drawn to the love of God in you. The authenticity of your individuality may not be accepted by all, but that's OK. "Fret not thyself!" The rejection of others or their lack of support does not negate the fact that you are a wonderful person in God's eyes with plans that He has divinely orchestrated.

If I were given permission to write an additional beatitude in the Bible, I would write, "Blessed are the uncool, for they shall be happy without needing the approval of others." I know that sounds little silly, but you get my point. You don't need to lower your standards just to raise someone else's opinion of you. Stop it! Instead, raise your standards and you will rise to see above their opinions. You may not be perfect and you may not always be Mr. or Ms. Popularity, but you are God's choice—ordained, sanctified, and called.

In conclusion, stop depending so much on people's input and instead "sell out," allowing God to have His way in your life. Choose to be ALL IN for Him with a made-up and stable mind-set![1]

10

MOVING PAST STUCK

The LORD our God spoke to us in Horeb, saying: "You have dwelt long enough at this mountain. Turn and take your journey, and go to the mountains of the Amorites, to all the neighboring places in the plain, in the mountains and in the lowland, in the South and on the seacoast, to the land of the Canaanites and to Lebanon, as far as the great river, the River Euphrates. See, I have set the land before you; go in and possess the land which the Lord swore to your fathers—to Abraham, Isaac, and Jacob—to give to them and their descendants after them."

—DEUTERONOMY 1:6–8

W E ALL KNOW the feeling of being stuck in traffic, an empty relationship, a dead-end job, a vehicle in the mud, or on an airplane that's just landed but the doors are still closed. I remember one time being on a plane that had just landed and being shoved by this "gentleman" (for lack of a better word) trying to move where there was no space. We were stuck, as the doors of the plane had not yet been opened, and here he was trying to create some momentum at my expense. I turned around and said, "Sir, shoving me won't help you get off any sooner." Thankfully, he got the hint and backed up a few steps and was better after that. It is common to sometimes feel like people are moving past us or moving up in life, yet here we are, living stuck.

Many of us are set in our ways, unwilling to change and stuck in our way of thinking. Staying stuck in our thinking prevents us from being ALL IN for God and is not healthy for our minds. It keeps us comfortable and safe rather than thriving and moving forward toward the future God has in store for us. Many live in their comfort zone, stay there, and die there! We live our lives like mushrooms—in the dark and surrounded by dung.

Nothing that is good can become stuck, and if it is stuck, it can't be any good! Stuck people want other people to stagnate with them—always remember to use wisdom when you choose those with whom you associate. We all have enormous potential (more than we can imagine), but sometimes we get stuck in unfruitful environments that limit or stunt our growth. Our "stinking thinking" causes us to focus more on our mistakes or what we've lost in the past than on the hope-filled future God has promised. Rather than living with hope, enthusiasm, and passion, we live in fear, worry, and regret. How can you be ALL IN when part of you is going backwards (at least mentally)? You can't move forward with your thoughts constantly dwelling on the past. It's time to RiseUp and move past neutral, move past stuck.

Moving past stuck requires us to understand that we need to walk in the will of God. Nothing outside of God's will is good for you. Vinegar and honey don't combine well; in fact, taking them at the same time might make you sick to your stomach. The same applies with a life "half in for God and half in for the world." Something will always be missing (we all know that miserable, empty feeling), which will cause you to wonder why you're not totally blessed, why you're not satisfied, and why you can't get past stuck. God gives us life, but it's up to us to make it good or bad. It's choice, not chance, that takes you past stuck into your divine destiny.

Some of us are not only stuck in dead-end jobs and toxic relationships, but we are stuck in the past and in our own comfort zone. One of the biggest enemies of human potential is being trapped in our comfort zone by life's problems or troubles wearing us down. I don't know about you, but I would rather be focused on my calling than my comfort zone. Why? Because focusing on my calling builds momentum and keeps me moving in the right direction. Lack of direction can not only get us into a rut but also stagnate our growth, which in turn can lead to unhealthy habits or paths.

As a pastor, one of the most important things I do for a couple about to be married is to provide them with premarital counseling. One of the subjects I address in the counseling sessions is how have they dealt with their past. I make sure that their "ex" has nothing to do with this "next" they're about to marry. It is imperative that this issue be dealt with before marriage.

As an energetic boy growing up, one of my favorite things on the playground was the monkey bars. I used to swing across them, back and forth, until my hands were sore. I think back to this because on the monkey bars, as in life, we must learn to let go of one thing in order to move forward. On the monkey bars, you can't progress to the next rung until you release the one you're holding. In life, we need to let go of past relationships to truly focus on a new one. In romantic relationships, it's one thing to be in love, but it's an entirely different thing to be stuck in a tainted love relationship heading nowhere. You become so obsessed and caught up in that lethal entanglement that you ignore all the signs of why you shouldn't be with that person.

Many continue going back and forth into the arms of their lovers when they know deep down they have no business being with them. It's not meant to be, but "stuckness" is present. Make sure you understand that being alone is better than being miserably yoked. And when the moment comes to consider the person you are courting for marriage, make sure they are aligned to your destiny and purpose. Marrying the wrong person will make you feel even more alone than if you were single. Therefore, do the will of God so you won't find yourself in stuck relationships.

In our walk of life, we can become complacent and drift away from God's will for us, thereby compromising His Word, which in turn leads us to consequences and situations that cause us to get stuck. We become so busy that our prayer time and times of solitude with Him shrink, leaving us uttering just emergency prayers so unlike our heartfelt and careful prayers from when we made time for Him. Before we knelt by our bedside and prayed with sincerity and purpose, but now we are too busy to pour out our hearts to Him.

Perhaps you have stopped reading God's Word, going to church consistently, or tithing. If so, you have entered into a compromising mind-set that conforms to worldly patterns and neglects what really matters, causing you to live in a stuck spiritual state. The spiritual world of God just doesn't intrigue you or seem real anymore. You don't sense His presence like before and you're out of sync, asking yourself, "What's happened to me? I feel awkward with God." You've drifted so far away that you now feel awkward or incapable of giving Him your precious time. You may have changed for the worse, but God always gives us the opportunity to reroute our steps.

One of the most powerful quotes I've ever read comes from General William Booth, who happens to have been the founder of the Salvation Army along with his wife, Catherine. He was quoted as saying this way back in the late 1800s: "The chief danger of the upcoming century will be religion without the Holy Ghost, Christianity without Christ, forgiveness without repentance, salvation without regeneration, politics without God, heaven without hell."[1] Was he on point or what? We are witnessing this in America right now with the "cotton candy satisfaction gospel" being preached in the pulpits—preaching that conveys lots of satisfaction but very little deliverance. Not many people are going to move past stuck this way.

For many of us, our enthusiasm was contagious the day we got saved, but now it has lost its steam or momentum. It seems as though modern Christianity doesn't want you to live on fire for God. The mentality is, "I'll go to church, but please don't challenge me to rise higher in my walk with Christ." The idea preached is to just keep drinking spiritual milk. Well, while milk is necessary for babies because it soothes and somewhat nourishes, at some point more substantial and challenging substances or meats have to be introduced. And while meats will challenge (you'll have to chew), that is what will bring transformation.

WAYS TO AVOID GETTING STUCK AND TO KEEP MOVING

1. STAY GROUNDED

> The righteous cry out, and the Lord hears,
> and delivers them out of *all* their troubles.

> The Lord is near to those who have a broken heart, and saves such as have a contrite spirit. Many are the afflictions of the righteous [which brings Stuck], but the Lord delivers him out of them *all*.
>
> —PSALM 34:17–19, EMPHASIS ADDED

Being grounded not only provides us with confidence, but it is also the place of default where we go when we are going through a really tough challenge. Fear is the glue that keeps you stuck, but faith is the solvent that sets you free. I don't know about you, but my help comes from the Lord Almighty.

2. SET YOUR HEART AND MIND ON PURE THINGS

> Set your minds on things that are above, not on things that are on earth.
>
> —COLOSSIANS 3:2, ESV

It's not what they say about you that matters; it's what you believe about yourself. Make sure you examine and guard your heart at all times while meditating on good things.

3. CHECK AND EXAMINE YOURSELF

> Examine yourselves as to whether you are in the faith. Test yourselves. Do you not know yourselves that Jesus Christ is in you?—unless indeed you are disqualified.
>
> —2 CORINTHIANS 13:5

In some cases, getting stuck could very well be the best thing that could happen to you. It can force you to stop the momentum of sin that is taking you down a wrong path, make you analyze your life, and cause you to end up seeking Jesus.

4. FLEE FROM THINGS OR PEOPLE THAT CAUSE YOU TO GET STUCK

> So humble yourselves before God. Resist the devil [that can't be too much fun, but it must be done], and he will flee from you. Come close to God, and God will come close to you. Wash your hands, you sinners; purify your hearts, for your loyalty is divided between God and the world.
>
> —JAMES 4:7–8, NLT

Some of you may be saying, "But Pastor Hery, I've already tried that and it didn't work!" Maybe you need to quit trying it your way and do it God's way, which means making up your mind, surrendering it all to Him, and suffering for a little (not permanent) while. Do you know the true definition of stubbornness? It's called insanity! When you do the same exact thing in your own strength but expect a different result. Everything that God created obeyed Him except man; even animals did their part. Therefore, simply obey the Word and let it move you past stuck.

5. STICK TO WHAT'S BIBLICAL

> All things are lawful for me, but not all things are helpful; all things are lawful for me, but not all things edify. Let no one seek his own, but each one the other's well-being.
>
> —1 CORINTHIANS 10:23–24

We need to get to a mature mind-set where opinions, and sometimes even facts, are not synonymous with God's divine TRUTH. Seek His knowledge and stop destroying yourself. It's so sad to see people seeking advice from horoscopes and questionable people instead of the Word of God. Can you imagine how much this world would be changed if believers would stick to what is biblical instead of what is popular or politically correct? I'm so tired of what is politically correct, a term used for overly sensitive people who want everything sugarcoated. We live for God's approval and to please Him, not people.

God wants to move us from milk to meats, from natural to supernatural, from conformed or comfortable to overcoming, from lack to abundance, and from stuck to progression. Eyes have not seen nor ears heard what God has in store for you. His eyes roam the earth to pour out His blessings, His favor, and His abundance on His people and His people's people. He wants to take you from nowhere to everywhere. He wants to take you from ordinary to extraordinary. He wants to help you RiseUp and rise higher. God will do His part, but you must do yours by moving forward in faith.

6. CHOOSE WHOM YOU WILL SERVE

> No one can serve two masters; for either he will hate the one and love the other, or else he will be loyal to the one and despise the other. You cannot serve God and mammon.
>
> —MATTHEW 6:24

Is God really "F.I.R.S.T." (F = Finances, I = Interests, R = Relationships, S = Schedule, and T = Trouble) in your life? It is easy to tell if you place God first or not in these five areas. Church, we have to make up our minds and decide who will be Lord of our lives. Understand this, my brethren: when you put God first, decisions become easier.

Don't let the enemy deceive you any longer; God works with brokenness and surrendered wills and blesses those who make Him Lord of lords. You won't have any regrets, I assure you, so why procrastinate? Procrastination will keep you from making lasting changes in your life. Procrastination rests on the assumption that you'll get another opportunity. Procrastination can be a big problem when it comes to important tasks or decisions being delayed or neglected, but it's disastrously worse when we dawdle in spiritual matters.

I once read an analogy on Christians that I found to be on point. It mentioned that there are three types of Christians: towboat Christians, sailboat Christians, and steamboat Christians. The towboat Christians never go forth unless somebody drags them along. The sailboat Christians will only venture in fair weather. But the steamboat Christians trust and proceed at all times. Church attendance and Christian fellowship are vitally important to the growth of our faith. This is very concerning—perhaps alarming—in light of present-day church attendance being so low. I've chosen to be like the warrior Joshua, who said (and I'm paraphrasing,) "I don't know about you all, but as for me and my house, we will serve the Lord" (Josh. 24:15). I'm ALL IN for God, and I want Him to keep using me for His glory. Do you want Him to use you mightily? Well, keep in mind that God will use and raise you to the next level only to the degree to which you keep dying to self.

7. MOVE ON TO WHAT IS NEXT (HOPE)

> Know that wisdom is such to your soul; if you find it, there will be a future, and your hope will not be cut off.
>
> —PROVERBS 24:14, ESV

> Do not remember the former things, nor consider
> the things of old. Behold, I will do a new thing.
>
> —ISAIAH 43:18–19

> Brethren, I do not count myself to have
> apprehended; but one thing I do, forgetting those
> things which are behind and reaching forward to
> those things which are ahead.
>
> —PHILIPPIANS 3:13

The three Bible verses above are strong anchors for those of us who desire to move forward past stuck. My brother or sister, if you are stuck in the past, just know that you cannot move forward while in reverse. Moses, who led his people out of Egypt and slavery, was a forward-thinking person and stood firm to God's command despite the Israelites' demands to return to Egypt. The Apostle Paul left behind many things as well (prestige, education, status) to serve His Savior. If all you want to know is what you already know, then you're already dying or stuck. "I don't mind this rathole, Pastor Hery; really, I'm fine!" No, you're not—at least, you won't be when you open your eyes and see how truly miserable you are! When we are denied oxygen, we perish. But newness in Christ, like spiritual oxygen, brings life and will get you going on a forward momentum! It will help you get back your passion, something that many of us have lost along the way. What is killing your passion, causing you to live stuck? It's safe to say that the very thing(s) you are holding on to and refusing to surrender to God is the thing(s) keeping you inhibited and stuck.

SEVEN PASSION KILLERS

1. UNCONFESSED AND DELIBERATE SIN

If we confess our sins, He is faithful and just to forgive us our sins and to cleanse us from all unrighteousness.

—1 JOHN 1:9

Many things can rob us of our joy, peace, confidence, focus, and passion for God, causing us to remain stuck. Sin brings shame and guilt, affecting our inner freedom. You may squeak into heaven, but you will have to pay a penalty for sin because the wages of sin is death (Rom. 6:23). We may say, "It's OK, everybody is doing it," but secretly we feel the guilt that is within us. No one can escape its cost or consequence. Truth be told, guilt will diminish the joy of passion. It's like going to Starbucks and ordering a bottle of Perrier water and a mocha coffee and alternating taking sips from each. It's just not going to taste right—the water will dilute the coffee, much like our guilt will dilute our passion.

Repentance, not remorse, is the key to operating in the fullness of His power. You may wonder, "What's the difference between the two?" Well, we feel remorse because we got caught. You apologize but eventually will go back to indulging your flesh. Whereas to feel genuine repentance means to suffer true regret about something and discontinue the action (or turn away from it). To do this, you have to give God your whole heart.

With my whole heart I have sought You; Oh, let me not wander from Your commandments! Your word I have hidden in my heart, that I might not sin against You.

—PSALM 119:10–11

Modern Christianity doesn't want people to know the Prince of Peace, they just want to sin in silence. Why do I say this? Why must I talk about sin? Why can't I just be like some of these other pastors that sermonize about God's love and hope? Simply because sin causes your passion for God to ebb, your tenacity to seek His face to fade and leave you complacent, your prayers to be hindered, and your Kingdom blessings to be delayed. I think those are all very good reasons to pound home this point! God's love is wonderful, but He is also a God of standards. You can't preach the four Gospels (Matthew, Mark, Luke, and John) that bring us the love of Jesus and omit the other sixty-two books in the Bible that speak about God's standards.

You have to get to the root cause in order to get out of your habitual stuck state. How can you produce good fruits if you don't have good roots? It's time to RiseUp and repent (turn away from your sin). Ask yourself: "Do I really want to play around with my salvation or eternal destination?" You want to make sure that once you depart from your earthly body, you will be with your Maker forevermore. I don't know about you, but I dislike flying standby. There's no guarantee you will have a seat on that plane. I prefer flying with a confirmed boarding pass and the confidence that I will have a place on that plane. The same applies to your eternity. Do you really want to take a gamble with your eternity flying on standby (assuming you're saved)? Eternity is too long to be wrong. Choose to have your confirmed seat, knowing that no matter what happens, heaven will be yours and you won't just squeak in.

Eternal salvation is important, but don't waste your life either. God has called you to be fruitful (obedience), not just busy, while you're still here on earth. If you don't like the fruit you are reaping in your life because you're in a stuck state, then change the seed you're sowing (behavior choices) in order to reap a rich and abundant harvest. But don't expect different results if you refuse to make changes!

2. Unresolved CONFLICT

> If you keep My commandments, you will abide in My love, just as I have kept My Father's commandments and abide in His love.
>
> —John 15:10

We need to walk in love more than conflict (trying to control others or questioning who's right). Conflict just drains the passion right out of you and brings resentment. I know what some of you may be thinking: "Let them off the hook? Why would I do that?" But listen carefully—I'm not telling you to let them off the hook. I'm telling you to put them on God's hook. Let them off *your* hook. Release the resentment. Not only will you allow yourself to emulate God's forgiving nature, but you will give people the grace to grow. Perhaps some of the people who hurt you are themselves hurting. You can show them God's love by showing them His grace through your act of forgiveness. Perhaps they don't have the same heart you do. You'll end up very disappointed if you go through life thinking people have the same heart as you. Not everyone knows the Lord. Forgiveness is the key when anger strikes and conflict arises. Demonstrate your spiritual maturity by turning the other cheek and putting the person in God's hands. Just say, "God, I can't handle this. Please take over, in Jesus's name!"

3. Unclear PURPOSE

> Then I said, "I have labored in vain, I have spent my strength for nothing and in vain."
>
> —Isaiah 49:4

Passion is what keeps you moving forward when your purpose is being questioned. Forgetting the purpose of your life is a sure way to kill your passion for life. Why get up from bed in the morning if you don't understand your purpose? Life without purpose is activity without direction. It's motion without direction. Passion and God's purpose go together!

4. UNUSED GIFTS AND TALENTS

> But the hour is coming, and now is, when the true worshipers will worship the Father in spirit and truth; for the Father is seeking such to worship Him. God is Spirit, and those who worship Him must worship in spirit and truth.
>
> —JOHN 4:23–24

An unused talent will cause you to lose your passion for life and passion for God. God gifted you to serve Him and to serve others. Gallup studies have shown that 70 percent of all Americans are in jobs that do not use their talents. This explains why so many people are walking around in utter frustration and discouragement.

5. UNBALANCED SCHEDULE (BALANCE IS CRUCIAL, AND THAT INCLUDES REST)

> There is no fear in love; but perfect love casts out fear, because fear involves torment. But he who fears has not been made perfect in love.
>
> —1 JOHN 4:18

How many of you claim to truly love God but live in fear? There can be no fear in love—they cannot exist simultaneously. Christians sometimes become afraid when they stop loving others, that is, when they look for the wrong in others rather than simply loving them. Love as God loves you, and you will see that fear recede.

Many people also believe that work, work, work is the answer. They work to offset their fears of failure, supply what they lack, and alleviate their worries. This is very common in today's society; too many of us have gotten caught up in the rat race. Understand that each day you will face all kinds of circumstances, distractions, and disappointments. But know that your heart follows hard after what it treasures! Make chasing after God a priority in your life despite your busyness.

6. UNSUPPORTED LIFESTYLE

> One thing I have desired of the LORD, that will I seek: that I may dwell in the house of the LORD all the days of my life.
>
> —PSALM 27:4

Sometimes you lose passion for God because you're not spending time with other people who have a passion for God—not fellowshipping with Christians or disciples. We need each other! Solitude may be refreshing, but isolation can be destructive. We are the church, and we cannot stop congregating (Heb. 10:25). We are the bride of Christ collectively, not individually or privately.

As a pastor, I see many people who have a passion for God totally lose that passion when spiritual attacks come against them. Many times, life's struggles cause us to return to our past. But God is trying to do a new thing in all of us, so we must press on. It's a very predictable pattern: no church attendance equates to a drop-in passion. Attending church online is wonderful, but don't make it your norm. It is meant for you to watch when you are ill, out of town, or when some other circumstance keeps you from your church home. We cannot make excuses for failing to congregate and depriving ourselves of the opportunity to feed off of each other's faith. That is a sure way to allow our hearts to get cold and harden.

7. UNDERNOURISHED SPIRIT (FORGETTING THE COST AT THE CROSS)

> And they said to one another, "Did not our heart burn within us while He talked with us on the road, and while He opened the Scriptures to us?"
>
> —LUKE 24:32

Let me ask you a question: Besides the sin of blasphemy, what is the worst sin in God's eyes? Adultery? Lying? Idolatry? He hates those, all right; however, I truly believe the sin of apathy—that is, lacking passion for God or loving Him half-heartedly—makes God's heart ache!

Many so-called Christians live with an attitude of, "Well, God is just one of the many things in my life. I also have a social life, a career, and my family obligations. So, I have this little slice of pie here called church, but only if I have time." Few things must stir God's wrath more than this. God response to that is, "How dare you? I am a jealous God who loves you and gave you My all!" Friends, He made you, breathed life into you, gifted you, purposed you, and saved you—and the best that you can offer Him is a slice of your life? You need to rethink that attitude—fast!

> Blessed are those who hunger and thirst for righteousness, for they shall be filled [satisfied, be filled, live passionately].
>
> —MATTHEW 5:6, EMPHASIS ADDED

Where there is hunger, there is passion; where there is passion, there is power!

Are you stuck today in a dead-end life where getting drunk or partying on weekends is your biggest happiness, like the old song by Loverboy, "Working for the Weekend"? Life is a lot more than that. If you're not living on purpose for God, you're stuck. Your mind is futilely spinning and you're unable to move forward—like when tires get stuck in mud—because life's answers are being concealed from you.

I encourage you to go from bitterness to sweetness and take the first step away from that lifestyle of emptiness and lack of purpose by chasing after the destiny and plans that God has in store for you. As you move forward toward your destiny, you will distance yourself from your history. If God were to reveal all His plans for you, you would be blown away! You would jump on board so fast and rush forward with His help. Don't spend all of your time trying to fix what's behind you; truthfully, it has already been said and done, and there is little you can do to fix it anyway. You have to trust God and move forward toward what He has in store. It's so much easier to steer through life with Him by your side.

In conclusion, we must understand and believe that God didn't give us a spirit of fear, but of power. It is perfect love, not demon-rebuking prayers, that casts out all fears. However, you need to have your love connection with God complete—forgive yourself and quit hanging on to things that need to be let go. The Apostle Paul told us that we are only restricted by our own passions. Therefore, break free and be ALL IN! This is not about praying a onetime prayer or admiring a baby in a manger, but about who is in the driver's seat of your life's journey. We either seek His presence or gradually drift away to the corruption and godless mind-set of this age. So ask yourself, who is going to govern your emotions, mind, and behavior? Are you going to have frustrations? Of course! Jesus never called you to be delivered from frustrations. However, He works, moves, and teaches in the midst of your frustrations.

People may see nothing of value inside you, but never forget that God's Holy Spirit is in there. He has made you to be more than a conqueror, which will enable you to move past stuck. His Word allows you to walk in freedom, but going against it will put you back in the muck and mire of a godless life. Freedom is not the right to do as we please, but to choose to do what is right. When we do what is right, we overflow with love, wisdom, joy, and peace. You don't have to wear a mask or pretend anymore, because when you are filled with the Holy Spirit inside, you don't have to fake anything on the outside. Now that's freedom! You are free from society's approval, free from guilt, and free from being stuck.

God is getting ready to refurbish and restore you into a new you. He wants to let you know that you can do all things through Christ because when you find out who you are in Him, you also discover what you have and stop responding to people and their opinions of you. So dig deeper, press through, and move forward, because God wants to set you free and release His supernatural power in you so that you can move past your stuck state. Choose to be ALL IN, and watch God move you!

11

ARE YOU A FAN OR A FOLLOWER?

And as He walked by the Sea of Galilee, He saw Simon
and Andrew his brother casting a net into the sea; for
they were fishermen. Then Jesus said to them, "Follow
Me, and I will make you become fishers of men." They
immediately left their nets and followed Him.

—MARK 1:16–18

TTEND ANY SPORTING event and you will witness
fans of all types rooting for their favorite team or
player, fans demonstrating their extreme passion
by their manner of dress (or costumes in some cases!) or
with their cheering and jumping up and down. Wouldn't
it be nice if they applied that same passionate intensity to
church, their prayers, or in their walk of faith? But while
many people are boisterous and devoted to their sports
teams, they are quiet and passive for Jesus Christ. They
focus their fanaticism on a team or player who, more than
likely, doesn't know or care about them. They worship
the creation more than the Creator. But Jesus Christ
is not looking for fans; He is looking for followers. As
the pressures of life increase and more distractions and

deadlines come at us, it becomes harder to live as Christ's disciples (spiritually disciplined) or as His followers.

Being a follower is much more than tithing, lugging around a heavy Bible, having a Christian song as your cell phone ringtone, or even having a Jesus fish bumper sticker on your car. What's the difference between being a fan and a follower of Jesus Christ? A follower is ALL IN—100 percent. Jesus wants all or nothing from us. He detests a lukewarm believer. The thought of a person calling himself a Christian without being a devoted follower of the Word of God is absurd.

I hope that this chapter will help some of you cross the one-yard line and experience the ultimate adventure that we experience when we surrender ALL IN to Jesus Christ. Keep in mind that a follower's goal is to be like Jesus (Luke 6:40) and to conform to His image (Rom. 8:29); therefore, we must acquaint ourselves with His Word. Followers have an intimate and personal knowledge of the one they follow. In other words, they know the person, they haven't just heard of him. The Word "know" in Hebrew is *Yada* (Gen. 4:1—"Now Adam knew Eve his wife"). Fans know about Jesus, but followers truly know Him.

Fans don't mind Jesus making some minor changes in their lives, but Jesus wants to turn our lives upside down! Fans don't mind Jesus doing a little touch-up work, but Jesus wants to perform a complete renovation and transformation. Followers, unlike the rich young ruler in Mark 10:17–22, fully surrender their hearts to Jesus Christ. In other words, one doesn't get saved or follow Jesus in small increments. Followers are ALL IN! As the Bible says in 2 Chronicles 16:9, "For the eyes of the LORD run to and fro throughout the whole earth, to show Himself strong on behalf of those whose heart is loyal [or surrendered] to Him."

Being a follower of Jesus Christ was not very popular during His time on earth; it isn't today, and it will become even more unpopular in the days to come. Heck, if social media would have existed when Jesus walked among us and when Adolf Hitler rose to power, Hitler definitely would have had more followers. Numbers can be deceptive, though. Hitler had his millions, but Jesus Christ had twelve, and with these twelve He changed the world for the better. Jesus is not concerned with numbers—look what He did with five loaves and two fish. He simply wants to know who is on His team and on that team willingly. Jesus doesn't force us to be on His team. It's your choice to either follow Him or, like most people, be a fan of Jesus the powerful historical figure.

So many people do not see Jesus as our Savior and exonerator of our sins. Many of us have a lukewarm opinion of Him despite the gruesome sacrifice He made for mankind. Life is full of phonies and fans; God certainly doesn't want any part of that. He wants you to come to Him with an open and sincere heart because that is what He desires and deserves. He wants you to follow Him passionately because He loves you passionately. He wants you to be a follower (disciple), not just a fan (casual believer).

Followers are people that follow Kingdom protocol. Followers listen to the Good Shepherd's voice. Followers are disciplined people. We are to discipline ourselves and grow for the purpose of godliness to be like Christ. In order for spiritual discipline to help us grow, the Holy Spirit's work must accompany us. However, we must be careful of the gradual compromises and time thieves that cause us to live careless rather than disciplined lives.

Personal discipline and spiritual discipline (Holy Spirit-led) work together to produce fruit in our lives. Just as we discipline ourselves to become godly, we must also always depend upon the Spirit to be fruitful. You may be thinking, "But pastor, I'm weak, I'm not strong enough, I'm not disciplined, blah blah." We are all weak without Holy Spirit assistance. Don't use your weakness or lack of discipline as an excuse, but choose instead to anchor your faith and hope in Christ Jesus. He will help you find a way as you choose to be a follower, not just His fan. Good intentions are not enough. We need to RiseUp and "just do it," because God has given you a conquering, powerful mind.

Have you ever wondered how a person who regularly attends church, serves joyfully, and lives on fire for God could all of a sudden, without any warning, fall into a sinkhole of sin? How could it be? Let me assure you it wasn't an overnight thing; more often than not, a lack in spiritual discipline was one of the main reasons for the fall. They may have gotten too busy, prayed fewer and fewer prayers, or began to compromise their devotional time, viewing it as a burden instead of a blessing. The enemy had them thinking that serving the Lord was all good and not much else was necessary. Not so. Their testimony or ministry became diluted because of one spiritual discipline compromise after another.

God understands we're busy! When you are a follower of Christ, it requires you to live prepared, not passive. It requires you to be committed, not just complacent. God wants followers, not just fans—people that are ALL IN for Him and are living disciplined lives.

IF YOU REALLY ARE A FOLLOWER
OF JESUS CHRIST, THEN . . .

THERE WILL BE RESULTS EVIDENT IN YOUR LIFE

In the Garden of Gethsemane, when Jesus's soul was deeply grieved and He was contemplating the cost of the Cross, He said, "Father, if it is possible, let this cup pass from Me; nevertheless, not as I will, but as You will" (Matt. 26:39). Many times, our flesh will desire to do what feels good, but a true follower of Jesus Christ will make the tough decision to follow God's will over their own. We will have many challenges and responsibilities in our lives, but doing His will brings us the results of priceless peace and joy. It's really your choice.

YOU ARE MORE THAN JUST A CHURCH MEMBER

Fans and followers worship differently. Fans think that a "religious" service is good enough. In other words, you wear the team jersey but have no part nor interest in the development of the team. Followers pursue Jesus more than self or others in a world that does just the opposite. Jesus doesn't want mind-to-mind ritual connectivity but heart-to-heart genuine connectivity. Rituals help you feel religious, but they don't make a difference in how you live. You have a religious experience but are still starving for joy, not to mention transformation of your heart, which seldom occurs. Unfortunately, many associate following Jesus with a myriad of rules, which results in them walking away from both church and a deep-rooted relationship with their Savior.

I have counseled distraught parents who said to me, "We raised him in church, Pastor!" to which I respond, "Excellent; but did you raise him in Christ?" Fans are the folks who only attend church but don't serve. They just show up. They don't really do much for Jesus, because they have other priorities. Singles—just because he or she regularly attends church doesn't make him or her an automatic potential mate for you. Satan goes there as well! Make sure he or she is in Christ as a follower, not a fan.

YOU WILL WALK MORE IN PEACE THAN IN STRIFE

> Therefore be imitators of God, as beloved children; and walk in love, just as Christ also loved you and gave Himself up for us, an offering and a sacrifice to God as a fragrant aroma.
> —EPHESIANS 5:1–2, NASB

If you have neither tolerance nor patience for others, you cannot claim you are following Jesus's teachings. If Jesus forgave those who crucified Him on the cross with nails, you have to learn to forgive those who have crucified you with words and evil deeds. Remember that forgiveness does not mean fellowship. You can have boundaries without resentment.

YOU WILL LOVE LIKE JESUS LOVED

> So he answered and said, "You shall love the LORD your God with all your heart, with all your soul, with all your strength, and with all your mind," and "your neighbor as yourself."
> —LUKE 10:27

There is no problem with the first command, but to be a follower you have to love others. Loving God is easy (He is perfect), but loving another imperfect human is not.

It's very difficult to live unhappy when you sow love, love, love! A follower loves like Jesus loved, lives like Jesus lived, and obeys the will of the Father (God's way). Therefore, lay down your life for your friends (John 15:13).

Choose to love God all out and never regret a day of your life! Fans are fair-weathered (what have you done for me lately?)—they go from hero to zero—but not Jesus Christ, your only constant. In other words, fans will bail out, give up, and walk away, but followers are ALL IN!

You will obey and are COMMITTED

> Then Jesus said to those Jews who believed Him, "If you abide in My word, you are My disciples indeed."
>
> —JOHN 8:31

All across America there are people, young and old alike, who are uncommitted. People who talk the talk but don't walk the walk. They live with a "conditional committed" mind-set. I'm no longer impressed with people who have the gift of gab but are not committed. Commitment is the bridge between what you know and what you do! In other words, commitment demands a choice! You must comprehend that until you are committed, you cannot win. Jesus wasted no time getting to the heart of commitment (follow or deny Me). I wonder what would happen if instead of wallowing in your "whatever" stage you threw your whole self into it. We are running out of time, excuses, and people to blame. To increase your effectiveness, make your emotions subordinate to your commitments. Understand that spiritual discipline and commitment builds character.

Hernán Cortés was a Spanish conquistador who led an expedition in the early sixteenth century that caused the fall of the Aztec Empire and brought large portions of mainland Mexico under new rule. Cortés was part of the generation of Spanish colonizers who began the first phase of the Spanish colonization of the Americas. One bold act of commitment was his order to burn the ships that brought them to the new world (point of no return). We conquer or we die. There were 11 ships, 110 sailors, and 553 soldiers (Spain really wanted to conquer Mexico).[1] His mind-set was "I may miss the mark, but I'm moving forward." How does this relate to this chapter? Fans applaud, but followers burn ships!

I would hate to have lived my entire life without ever knowing what I could have been had I not been committed to anything. Commitment requires sacrifices, not just benefits; and followers are committed, not just involved! Let me put that into a scenario to which we can all relate—breakfast. In the typical breakfast meal of bacon and eggs, the hen (eggs) is involved, but the pig (bacon) is committed. Fans stay as long as it benefits them, but if it doesn't benefit them, they won't hang. As long as they're happy, they'll show up, but they get easily offended when they can't get their own way and leave. Followers will stay true to Jesus all the way to Glory.

Are you truly saved? Are you really a follower? If yes, then you will go the distance! Revelation 2:10 says, "Do not fear any of those things which you are about to suffer. Indeed, the devil is about to throw some of you into prison, that you may be tested, and you will have tribulation ten days. Be faithful until death, and I will give you the crown of life."

YOU WILL NOT BE ASHAMED OF JESUS OR THE GOSPEL

> For I am not ashamed of the gospel of Christ, for it is the power of God to salvation for everyone who believes, for the Jew first and also for the Greek.
>
> —ROMANS 1:16

People can be very daring on social media (Facebook, Twitter, texting, etc.) and behind the wheel, but they are nowhere near as bold and courageous when it really counts. They comply or conform to the world's standards rather than RiseUp to represent Christ well and share the gospel as He desires. Being bold and courageous as we witness or share the gospel is paramount. People need the filling of the Holy Spirit to bring additional boldness to their walk with God. The disciples were a bunch of cowardly common men before the Holy Spirit's manifestation arrived. People went from being weaklings to being mighty warriors of God's Word preaching to thousands, laying hands on the sick, and casting out demonic spirits in Jesus's mighty name. Therefore, it's safe to say that while fans received the gift of the Holy Spirit, it was the followers who were filled with the Holy Spirit. I elaborate on this further in Chapter 16.

You will KNOW Him (the Blesser) and not just know of Him (to get blessings)

> And this is eternal life, that they may know You, the only true God, and Jesus Christ whom You have sent.
>
> —John 17:3

Fans want the blessings, but followers want the Blesser. Some people love Jesus as long as He is like a butler, a shadow on whose face they never really focus. Some of us are so busy that we don't have time to seek His face and we procrastinate on what truly matters: knowing Him more. We are more concerned about our own business than the business of the Lord. Please listen to me, friend; if you're too busy for God, you're too busy! You are doing yourself a disservice. He is the Bread of Life and the Living

Water, yet instead of receiving this true nourishment, we gorge ourselves with donuts that will ultimately leave us unfulfilled and dissatisfied.

Many people in our society suffer unnecessarily because they are hungry—spiritually hungry. They try out different faiths, cults, or belief systems but are never satisfied! Something is always missing in their lives. There is a deep void and emptiness within them that causes them increased anxiety, and they make wrong choices trying to fill it. So how does one get spiritually full? Jesus said that we will find spiritual fulfilment only by coming to Him (as a follower); nothing else will do. Jesus said in Matthew 4:4, "It is written, 'Man shall not live by bread alone, but by every word that proceeds from the mouth of God." Many are settling for bread crumbs rather than the whole loaf. The Word of God is meant to be bread for daily nourishment, not cake for special occasions. People ask at the dinner table for someone to pass them the butter, salt, or pepper; but these days it seems like many are saying, "Please pass the crumbs!" That sounds awkward, right? God probably thinks the same thing.

In Matthew 14:13–21, we read about how Jesus fed more than five thousand people. But the very next day, many of those people were still looking for something else or something more. Obviously "something" was missing in their lives! That's the difference between a fan and a follower. Followers are content and satisfied, or at least they should be. But many of us think we can live a fulfilled life of priceless peace, joy, and inner freedom eating crumbs. The Word will keep you from sin, and sin is going to keep you from the Word. Picky eaters (fans) of God's Word will never be filled or fulfilled by the fullness of God.

The Bread of Heaven (Jesus Christ) is not a stuffy religion but a person. You can't be saved by yourself or by some religion; salvation only comes through Jesus and Jesus alone. The Word says in Acts 4:12, "There is salvation in no one else! Under all heaven there is no other name for men to call upon to save them" (TLB). Jesus conquered death and that is what separates Him from all other mediators or co-mediators.

Man can try any method of salvation he chooses. That is one of the great privileges of being a human—God has created us with free will. We have the ability to choose how we will live our lives. However, regardless of how a man lives or what path he chooses for his life, salvation, perfect peace, unspeakable joy, and true fulfillment will only come through Jesus Christ!

We need to stop seeing Jesus as our copilot, sugar daddy, or genie. He is not a hobby or a trend, nor is He a symbolic or a fire-escape type of god. He is the Bread of Life, not the bread of strife! He can be trusted, and He will never fail you. What are you holding on to that is preventing you from being ALL IN? Why are you fighting to stay in control when real inner freedom only comes when you surrender control (your will) to His will? The energy of surrender accomplishes much more than the energy of control. Trying to live the "good life" according to your terms and outside of His perfect will is a guaranteed path to frustration, discouragement, and closed doors. Jesus is enough to bring fullness to your life! Discard the bread crumbs and go seek the Bread of Life that will help you produce good fruit. It will cost you, though; it's not for the lame. Just because salvation is free to receive, this doesn't mean that it won't cost you something to walk in the power of God. Fans don't pay much of a price, but then again, they won't receive the fullness of His blessings. Followers pay a price, but the rewards are breathtaking!

Don't be fooled: if you settle for crumbs as a fan rather than trusting in God your protector and provider as a follower, the enemy will constantly try to remind you of what you could have had or could have been. If crumbs are all you expect, then that's what you'll have. If half-hearted peace as a fan is what you want, that's what you'll have. That could have been then, but this is now! God's about to open heaven on you. The past does not disqualify you from future miracles.

Let me warn you right here and now: some people will only like you when you're eating crumbs, and the moment you RiseUp to Bread, they will start to envy you. Always remember to please God, not people; seek His approval, not men's opinions. Learn to be satisfied in Him, but not so satisfied that you take your foot off the pedal. Sometimes it is dangerous to be too satisfied! I would rather be desperately and tenaciously chasing after the Bread of Life—my Savior, Master, and Lord—than the crummy options this world offers.

Some of you may be in a crummy situation, crummy marriage, crummy job, crummy health situation, or earning a crummy income—to put it bluntly, you're living a pretty crummy life. I'm here to tell you that God is not finished with you yet. As long as you are breathing, there is purpose in your life. Surrender to the Bread of Life and stop settling for crumbs. Choose to be His follower and not just a fan!

Elevation and promotion will come as you dine at the table of Lord! You need to RiseUp and get yourself together despite the obstacles. You need to say, "Can you please pass me the Bread?" Reach for the Bread that brings life! Reach for the Bread that will restore your marriage, bless you with a better job, provide for you, improve your health, heal your body, and bring life to your soul.

God said, "I Am Who I Am" (Exod. 3:14), meaning "I Am Light, I Am Love, I Am Life, I Am your Shepherd, I Am your Comforter, I Am your Healer, I Am your Counselor, I Am your Savior, I Am your King, I Am your Redeemer; I Am the Bread of Life that satisfies!" Unlike the manna wafers that God provided for Moses to give to the Israelites in the desert, this Bread never crumbles or spoils. What a gift! Yet people continue to search for things that moth and rust can destroy.

Perhaps you're lacking in something and don't even know what it is. Listen—God is telling you, "I Am here for you!" You will never go hungry or thirsty when you eat of the Bread of Life and drink the Living Water (Jesus)! My friend, the Word of God says we can't serve two masters (Matt. 6:24). Choose today to follow Him and stop short-changing yourself. The ultimate gift in life is not the mansions, money, boats, cars, and so forth. The ultimate gift is the presence of God the Father in Jesus Christ, and now He's in you. Apart from Him you are nothing, but if you remain in Him you will experience utmost satisfaction! Spending time with Jesus helps you live less arrogantly, less worried, less anxious, less fearful, less lustful, and more complete.

Listen, there are not many things in life that are guaranteed. We do not know what will happen under our new president's administration. We do not know what will happen with the economy nor how it will affect our 401K—but we do know with certainty that with Jesus we shall have life!

Are you willing today to say, "Father God, where You lead me, I will follow"? God does something in the supernatural spiritual world when we cry out and say, "Father God, I'm ALL IN; have Your way in me!" Understand, though, that if you are going to be a follower, it takes the choice out of it. You simply are going to lay your life down for God and entrust your whole life to Him. You don't want to leave it to chance or fate; you really have to know Him.

Look at what the Bible says in Matthew 7:21–23:

> Not everyone who says to Me, "Lord, Lord," shall enter the kingdom of heaven, but he who does the will of My Father in heaven. Many will say to Me in that day, "Lord, Lord, have we not prophesied in Your name, cast out demons in Your name, and done many wonders in Your name?" And then I will declare to them, "I never knew you; depart from Me, you who practice lawlessness!"

That's just too much of a risk for me, but a fan will foolishly bank on it. A true follower, however, will turn to God and do His will.

NAVY SEAL DISCIPLESHIP

A true follower or disciple is ALL IN! I'm not referring to a fan Christian who believes in Jesus Christ as Lord but not Savior and eventually sells out. I like to compare a true follower to a Navy SEAL, one of the most prestigious positions in the military. They endure rigorous and gruesome training for the purpose of developing not only physical strength and stamina, but mental strength. Most people who are accepted into the training program quit and can never claim this admirable and prestigious title.

One of the main principles the SEAL learns is self-denial. Self-denial is key to being not only a successful Navy SEAL but also a good disciple. In the spiritual sense, it is impossible to be a disciple (follower) of Christ and still be in charge. We must relinquish control to Him. Unfortunately, not enough pastors preach this from the pulpit.

Let me explain spiritual self-denial, if I may. You've accepted Jesus as your Savior; you've crossed the line from being a non-believer to being a believer, or from doubt to faith. Your sins had separated you from God, but now you have been reconnected to Him. Congrats! What's next? Becoming a disciple (disciplined follower) so Jesus can now also be your Lord (have priority in your decision making). We have to be trained like a soldier or athlete. I love what the Bible says in 1 Corinthians 9:24–27 (ESV):

> Do you not know that in a race all the runners run, but only one receives the prize? So run that you may obtain it. Every athlete exercises self-control in all things. They do it to receive a perishable wreath, but we an imperishable. So I do not run aimlessly; I do not box as one beating the air. But I discipline my body and keep it under control, lest after preaching to others I myself should be disqualified.

God Almighty is in the search for followers who demonstrate real discipleship. He desires people with excellent character and a heart for the gospel, humble servants that love Him in spirit and in truth.

TEN QUALITIES OF A NAVY SEAL DISCIPLE

1. PASSIONATELY COMMITS TO FOLLOWING JESUS

Making Jesus your Savior and Lord; falling more and more in love with Him. Some people are going to miss heaven by mere inches (they have John 3:16 in their minds but not in their hearts). Salvation was never meant to be contained. Commit today to get closer to Him!

2. EMBRACES THEIR IDENTITY (WITHOUT UNNECESSARY ADDED PRESSURE)

God is not going to ask why you weren't like Moses or David, but why didn't you do you? Lack of identity is the root of insecurity! You only become jealous, prideful, and insecure when you don't see your own calling and potential in God.

3. EVALUATES LIFE ACCORDING TO BIBLICAL STANDARDS, NOT EMOTIONS OR OPINIONS

The Bible is our manual not only for renewing our mind but also for enabling us to speak in the language of God. The Word of God has the power to release the very life that's inside of God. When we speak the Word, we're not just speaking with an audible voice; we are literally speaking spirit and life. The more you do that, the more the spirit of the Word will transform your life.

4. IS SENSITIVE AND SUBMITS TO THE HOLY SPIRIT

> For all who are led by the Spirit of God are sons [disciples] of God.
>
> —ROMANS 8:14, ESV

How do we do this?

- Submit to what the Holy Spirit is SAYING

> And he said to them, "Pay attention to what you hear: with the measure you use, it will be measured to you, and still more will be added to you."
>
> —MARK 4:24, ESV

This is the secret to increased sensitivity and the key to hearing more of God's voice. The sheep should never be offended by the voice of their good Shepherd.

- Become a WORSHIPPER of God (create an atmosphere conducive to receiving the Holy Spirit)

While they were worshiping the Lord and fasting, the Holy Spirit said, "Set apart for me Barnabas and Saul for the work to which I have called them."

—ACTS 13:2, ESV

God thrives on worship. We cannot overworship God. He provides favor to us when we worship Him in spirit and in truth.

- Draw CLOSER to God (don't allow anything to replace devotion time).

You make known to me the path of life; you will fill me with joy in your presence, with eternal pleasures at your right hand.

—PSALM 16:11, NIV

When you draw closer to God, four things happen: 1) Sin is revealed; 2) God's will is made known; 3) your soul is calmed; and 4) you continue to grow closer to Him.

5. Lives MORALLY (PURE IN BODY, HEART, AND MIND)

And everyone who thus hopes in him purifies himself as he is pure.

—1 JOHN 3:3, ESV

A Navy SEAL embraces the commands of his superiors. The same applies to a disciple of the Most High. The commands of God cannot be optional regardless of what you may be going through. Why? Because obeying these commands is the only thing that will give life to your circumstances.

6. Dedicates themselves to a HEALTHY family

> But as for me and my household, we will serve the LORD.
>
> —JOSHUA 24:15, NIV

No one will roast you harder than your own family, but I believe if you serve God with an ALL IN mind-set (balanced, of course), He will turn your house into a home. Our cell phones have already replaced our cameras, calendars, and alarm clocks; don't let it replace your family.

7. Becomes engaged in HELPING their community and bridging culture gaps

Allow me to encourage you to give your *heart* to God and your *hands* to mankind. We experience such inner joy when we help, give, and serve. I keep discovering the power of God in my life when I do things for other people. God does not comfort us to make us comfortable; He comforts us to make us comforters. Be there for others, but never leave yourself behind. And remember, the things that you do for Jesus are the only things that will last.

8. Evangelizes BOLDLY and COURAGEOUSLY (gospel witnessing and/or serving)

> But you will receive power when the Holy Spirit has come upon you, and you will be my *witnesses*

in Jerusalem and in all Judea and Samaria, and
to the end of the earth.

—ACTS 1:8, ESV, EMPHASIS ADDED

The closer you are to God, the more boldness and
confidence you will have. King Saul drifted from God and
was afraid of Goliath. The further you are from God, the
bigger your Goliath looks. Disciples (followers) get closer
and closer to God!

9. LIVES WITH A RESPONSIBLE MISSION OR PURPOSE

And we know that all things work together for
good to those who love God, to those who are
the called according to His *purpose.*

—ROMANS 8:28, EMPHASIS ADDED

For I know the thoughts that I think toward you,
says the LORD, thoughts of peace and not of evil,
to give you a future and a hope.

—JEREMIAH 29:11

Everything in life was created to solve a problem, but
only purpose will bring ultimate fulfillment. In America,
your purpose may not pay you well. Our culture pressures
us and tells us that money, fame, and power bring
fulfillment. Many embrace this idea with little thought
only to end up restless and stressed down the road. We
chase the money not realizing that we can only experience
maximum fulfillment by following God's purpose.
Unfortunately, many will leave their purpose, die without
embracing it, and chase the mighty dollar—then wonder
why they aren't happy.

If money was not an issue, what would you be doing with
your life? This is an indicator of your divine assignment

(mission or purpose). Your job is what you do, but who you are (purpose) is different. We must know that man's system is not synonymous with God's system. Ask God in prayer to help you discover the purpose of your existence, because the purpose of life is to discover your gift and the meaning of life is to give your gift away.

10. Is dedicated to acquiring WISDOM (spiritual maturity)

> I fed you with milk and not with solid food; for until now you were not able to receive it, and even now you are still not able.
> —1 Corinthians 3:2

> If any of you lacks wisdom, let him ask of God, who gives to all liberally and without reproach, and it will be given to him.
> —James 1:5

God Almighty doesn't want us to remain the same. He desires for us to go from glory to glory, changing and transforming to the likeness of His Son. He wants us to grow and mature in Christ and to occupy with authority, dominion, and power! He doesn't just want you to have your "ticket to heaven" and remain worldly or fleshly in your life here on earth. His glory shall cover the earth, and you are His representative. I am declaring in the name of Jesus that you are the interruption of any curse in your bloodline; therefore, align to the divine! Choose to be a disciple—a follower of the Bread of Life, not just a believer who settles for the crumbs.

A Believer Versus a Disciple

A Believer believes in Jesus as Savior but lives to please self.

A Disciple believes in Jesus as Lord and lives to please God.

A Believer promotes his opinions, feelings, and thoughts above the Word of God.

A Disciple exalts the Word of God above his opinions, feelings and thoughts.

A Believer thinks of church as a place where she hears what God's Word says.

A Disciple thinks of church as a place where she learns to do what God's Word says.

A Believer is accountable only to himself and serves God based on convenience.

A Disciple is accountable to everyone and serves God based on conviction.

A Believer seeks to know God through religion.

A Disciple seeks to know God through relationship.

A Believer follows God as long as everything is going well.

A Disciple follows God regardless of the circumstances.

A Believer chooses her own path and asks God to bless it.

A Disciple asks God to choose her path and follows it.

A Believer puts entertainment, career, and relationships ahead of God in his daily life.

A Disciple puts God first in his daily life.

A Believer follows the example of the world and seeks elevate her importance.

A Disciple follows the example of Jesus and seeks to become subservient.

12

BE LIKE CHRIST

Therefore be imitators of God as dear children.
And walk in love, as Christ also has loved us
and given Himself for us, an offering and a
sacrifice to God for a sweet-smelling aroma.
—EPHESIANS 5:1–2

GOD'S ULTIMATE DESIRE for us is not that we engage in prayer or moral living, but that we become more like Him, representing Him favorably as ambassadors of His kingdom. Christians are people who are called to represent the living God in a world that has no clue who He is. Regrettably, those who claim to know Him best oftentimes represent Him in the least positive manner. Spiritual growth is not about doing more; it's about becoming more like Jesus. It's not about liking Jesus, but about being more like Jesus. You have to be rooted in the identity of Christ and not popular opinions.

Unfortunately, the world has a very negative view or opinion of Christians. As a matter of fact, according to the Barna Group, the top five words with which the world describes Christians are 1) judgmental; 2) unforgiving;

3) insensitive; 4) homophobic; and 5) hypocritical. These words do not represent or describe our Lord Jesus Christ! The Bible says in 1 John 2:6, "He who says he abides in Him ought himself also to walk just as He walked." To a great degree, your friends determine who you are. Following that train of reasoning, if you are in a friendship with your Maker, you will be like Christ.

Do you consider yourself a picky food eater? I'm not, but my wife somewhat is. I can eat pretty much anything, but she usually keeps it safe by having the same foods. In the spiritual realm, "picky eaters" of God's Word will never be satiated by the fullness of God. Why? Because the likeness of Christ will not mature in them nor bring them transformation. They will live their lives conforming rather than transforming. His Word in Galatians 4:19 tells us, "My little children, for whom I labor in birth again until Christ is formed in you." God is going to open up some new doors in your life. He's going to make a way where there seems to be no way. But your decision has to be, "God, I'm all in! I want to be like Christ!"

How do we become more like Christ? By tapping into the Wonderful Counselor who is the Holy Spirit. He knows our destiny and operates in us much like a navigational system. God prepares you for the turns of life despite the busyness of your life just like a navigational system works despite traffic. A navigational system is silent when we are headed in the right direction. There is no need for correction or direction; it's all good as we drive forward. Instruction is given to turn right or turn left or to continue for another three miles. If we want to get to our destination quickly and safely, we do as it instructs. The nudges of the Holy Spirit should also be taken seriously and adhered to so that we can stay on the straight and narrow path that leads to a more abundant life.

There will be many times when God is silent; the question is, can you trust Him in the silence? Psalm 18:30 says, "As for God, His way is perfect; the Word of the LORD is proven; He is a shield to all who trust in Him." We miss out on God's best for us and suffer unnecessarily when we are outside His perfect will. The Holy Spirit guides us into all truth and keeps us on the path that will produce fruit in our lives. It is prudent in this hurried and confusing world that we seek the Lord daily to gain a sense of His direction for our lives—not only so that we know where He wants us to go, but also so we can exemplify Him in our day-to-day lives.

Isn't it fantastic to know that if you miss a turn, God knows how to reroute your journey? When we make a wrong turn while driving, our navigational system will say "rerouting." If you are open to Him, God will do the same when we make wrong life choices. Though we will pay the penalty or consequence of sin (no one can escape that), I am thankful that He will do everything possible to help us make the right turns (choices). His mercy never ceases to amaze me; indeed, his mercies are new each day. We just need to stay in step rather than continuing to step out of line. Some people have made so many wrong choices that they feel they are beyond God's help. But God is ready to help you reroute your course despite your past. Notice, however, that I said "help." Ultimately, it's up to you to make the right turns or choices that will bring you the spiritual maturity you need to justly represent Him!

The Cross represents more than just our Savior dying and shedding His innocent blood in atonement for our sins. The Cross should also represent a life of restraint from sin that causes us to live incomplete, unfulfilled, and dissatisfied lives. This Christian walk of ours is a life of spiritual discipline. No one has ever truly matured in the spiritual sense unless they have applied themselves to spiritual discipline. Discipline determines destiny!

I hear people say how difficult or challenging it is to develop and/or maintain their body, mind, marriage, or studies. Nothing good comes easy—we might as well accept this! An undisciplined lifestyle may seem (and may start out) easy, but it comes with a price of failure and regret. Living a Christlike life will not be easy, but its rewards will be plentiful, and it will get you exactly where you need to be and make you who you need to be.

Seven Ways We Can Be More Like Christ

1. Walk in LOVE (prosper in your relationships; Forgive)

> Therefore, as the elect of God, holy and beloved, put on tender mercies, kindness, humility, meekness, longsuffering; bearing with one another, and forgiving one another, if anyone has a complaint against another; even as Christ forgave you, so you also must do. But above all these things put on love, which is the bond of perfection.
>
> —Colossians 3:12–14

The way the world will know we are followers of Jesus is by our love, by the way we walk in His likeness and without a spirit of condemnation (wrong judgement). Many want to share the truth but don't do so with love. On the other hand, many preach about His love but not His standards. The fact of the matter is that truth without love is brutality and love without truth is hypocrisy. We have to balance His truth with His love or else the message is totally ineffective.

It is so crazy that some people think we can guilt others into getting saved. The love of God covers us in grace and directs us to a better future; it has no need for condemnation. But perhaps you were first introduced to the gospel by someone who preached without love and you carry the hurt you suffered from that person's judgment. Here's your chance to be more like Jesus—forgive them! For all you know, they did their best with what they knew. Church-hurt is sometimes the worst, because it leaves you paralyzed in astonishment. You tend to think that churchgoers should know better.

Don't put your trust in man, but solely in God. Know that Jesus Christ is the only role model on whom you should focus, and simply accept the fact that humans will fall short.

2. Walk in TRUTH

> I have no greater joy than to hear that my children walk in truth.
>
> —3 John 1:4

Those who fear God believe God's Word regardless of their circumstances. Don't try to fool Him; Jesus deals better with imperfections than with deceptions. The truth, not perfection, sets you free! Where truth is not present, Christ is absent. Truth is not based on human opinions or traditional culture patterns, nor is it rooted in logic. None of those things have authority when it concerns spiritual matters.

In our judicial court system, the US Supreme Court is the absolute authority. Much to that effect, the Word of God is the absolute authority—certainly not our feelings or opinions. Our feelings may be authentic, but that doesn't mean they are the truth! Be real and truthful with yourself, because being a fake is just too exhausting. When we are not people of truth, our energy disappears, our character decays, and our integrity depreciates. Our souls can only find rest in the truth!

3. WALK IN GRACE

> And the Word became flesh and dwelt among us, and we beheld His glory, the glory as of the only begotten of the Father, full of grace and truth.
> —JOHN 1:14

We all love to receive grace, but most of us struggle with showing it to others. We want grace for us but justice for them. Rather than extending grace and giving people the opportunity to grow, we are quick to ask God to exact His vengeance on them. Why preach grace, then? Because Jesus came as a lifeguard to rescue, redeem, and restore us back to Himself. He wants us to be like Him, not—to reference the old Gatorade ads—like Mike. Be a life preserver to someone today and share the gospel of grace with them in truth and in love.

4. WALK IN WISDOM (JESUS GREW IN WISDOM, AND HE WAS A DISCIPLINED MAN)

> And Jesus increased in wisdom and stature, and in favor with God and men.
> —LUKE 2:52

In order to acquire wisdom, we must be exceptional hearers and doers. The devil will try to keep you busy and focused on things that really don't matter in the grand scheme of life. He will get you so distracted that it will feel as though you're walking around with headphones listening to his lies, becoming less and less able to hear the Lord's voice. He will try to take your motivation from you so that you don't put God first! We have to prioritize and stay focused on the things that truly matter.

We have to situate ourselves in a position to succeed by God's means, because position matters. Martha was distracted by her preparations, but Mary positioned herself at the Lord's feet in order to hear instructions. Who was wiser? Who prospered in her soul? Isn't it funny how we become so busy securing the things of our material world, which are temporary and will fade, but miss out on securing the spiritual things that are eternal and cannot be taken away? Matthew 7:24–27 says:

> Therefore whoever hears these sayings of Mine, and does them, I will liken him to a wise man who built his house on the rock: and the rain descended, the floods came, and the winds blew and beat on that house; and it did not fall, for it was founded on the rock. But everyone who hears these sayings of Mine, and does not do them, will be like a foolish man who built his house on the sand: and the rain descended, the floods came, and the winds blew and beat on that house; and it fell. And great was its fall.

Growing in godliness means growing in wisdom in order to obtain God's divine favor. We all have gifts, but talent without wisdom is not prudent. We need both! It needn't be anything as drastic as immoral behavior— any behavior that puts us out of the will of God is unwise. We don't want to be just "good" people; we want to be wise people who represent Jesus Christ with the right actions, not just empty words. That's wisdom!

5. WALK IN FAITH (POWER OF YOUR WORDS AND IN YOUR GIVING)

> For we walk by faith, not by sight.
>
> —2 CORINTHIANS 5:7

Our walk with God is not just about growing in faith, but about making our faith all-encompassing. So many Christians struggle with their faith. They constantly wonder if it's big or strong enough. They walk around doubting themselves and with a mind-set of unbelief. Jesus gave us these six powerful words in Mark 5:36, "Do not be afraid; only believe." That is a truth that we should engrave in the core of our hearts. We should be a church that represents the body of Christ by praying in faith, eating in faith, walking by faith, and seeing by faith. No amount of standard human learning is an effective substitute. The righteous shall live by faith and not just reasoning.

6. WALK IN THE SPIRIT

> I say then: Walk in the Spirit, and you shall not fulfill the lust of the flesh. For the flesh lusts against the Spirit, and the Spirit against the flesh; and these are contrary to one another, so that you do not do the things that you wish.
>
> —GALATIANS 5:16–17

The Holy Spirit is not a something but a someone. He is one of the three persons of the Trinity and is the One who will help us become like Jesus Christ. The word "spiritual" does not necessarily mean Spirit-filled; it means Spirit-led. When we are led by the Spirit, restoration—not condemnation—is our destiny.

7. WALK IN SUBMISSION

For I have come down from heaven, not to do
My own will, but the will of Him who sent Me.
—JOHN 6:38

While He walked the earth, Jesus endured many temptations, but He resisted all of them by submitting His entire life to the Father. That included making time for solitude in prayer and fasting. It is impossible to be like Christ and have our way! There is no way Jesus could have done all that He did in public without lots of prayers in private whereby He surrendered Himself to His Father's perfect will. It's one thing to ask God for an answer to your prayer, but it's another to submit to the answer with which He responds—just as it's one thing to ask Him for direction but another to follow His way!

The prefix "sub" means to go under, and the word "mission" comes from the Latin word meaning "to send." We are to go under the One who has sent us to be the light of the world. Our plans, purposes, and dreams must be submitted to His perfect will. This will bring us the utmost joy, but it will also bring a tug in our flesh. This is why submission to His perfect will is vital. On the other hand, a mind that is set on the flesh is hostile toward God's will and God's people, thus it cannot submit as Christ did to His Father.

As I've mentioned before, many Christians want to have "fire insurance" to keep them out of hell but do not live with Jesus Christ as Lord of their lives. They might get into heaven because they acknowledge Jesus as their Savior, but they do not rank Him important enough to live a life surrendered to Him. They are vampire Christians who want the blood but not His lordship!

The fact of the matter is that failing to submit to Him will leave us open to the lies, myths, and traps of the enemy! Failing to submit will leave us unfulfilled, incomplete, and lacking in joy. I'm talking about the type of joy that gives you strength and inner passion, and helps you come alive. It is not dependent on external factors. Joy—unlike happiness, which never gives what it promises—helps you live with rivers of living water inside your soul like Jesus lived. How can you know all this and still be half-hearted about God? Can't you see how much you will miss out on when you're not ALL IN for Christ?

Listen—Jesus is coming back, and from all the fulfilled prophecies going on in our own time, I venture to say sooner rather than later. He is coming for a church (us) without blemishes or wrinkles. He is not coming back to a "Hey, let me live my life as I choose to live" mind-set. He's not coming back for a defeated, failing, or discouraged church. He is coming back for a glorious, holy, and Christlike bride. You may feel unworthy, guilty, and ashamed because of your past or even your present lifestyle, but you can turn (repent) from it and begin living ALL IN for Him, effective immediately.

Just because your past has been damaged or has lacked joy, this doesn't mean your future has to be the same. No one is perfect, but here is some really good news: God doesn't need for you to present your perfect self to Him; He wants you to present your real self to Him. In fact, God doesn't even want to remember your sins. Micah 7:19 says, "He will again have compassion on us, and will subdue our iniquities. You will cast all our sins into the depths of the sea [Sea of Forgetfulness]." If God forgets, who are we to remember? It is great to know there are no black sheep in His kingdom. Jesus was real with His struggles to God, and you can be too. Life is full of pretention and insincerity, and God certainly doesn't want any part of that. Just come to Him with an open and sincere heart.

PART 4

STANDING STRONG

PART 4

STANDING STRONG

13

THE BATTLE IS NOT YOURS

And he said, "Listen, all you of Judah and
you inhabitants of Jerusalem, and you, King
Jehoshaphat! Thus says the LORD to you: 'Do
not be afraid nor dismayed because of this great
multitude, for the battle is not yours, but God's.'"
—2 CHRONICLES 20:15

ONE THING I'VE learned, and in some ways am
still learning, is that not every battle is worth
fighting. We have to ask ourselves, even if we
win the battle, what long-term benefit will the win bring
us? If we constantly engage in every battle, then we will
not have the energy to fight the battles that really do
matter. We are not supposed to be in "fight mode" all of
the time. Here we are, getting all out of focus trying to
win over all of our critics and haters, getting angry, and
losing our peace. We don't have to fight *mano a mano*
when we have a powerful God, His Son who intercedes
for us, and a mighty kingdom army of angels fighting in
the spiritual realm for us. The victory is already ours, but
know that the battle belongs to the Lord.

In the Bible, David was a true champion because he knew which battles to fight. He knew he had to bring his God into the mix. He knew the reward and what was at stake when he chose to fight Goliath. David's battle was worth the fight because Israel was being threatened by this Philistine giant. David ran at Goliath shouting out, "You come at me with a spear and a sword, but I come against you in the mighty name of Jehovah God of Israel!" When the enemy silences you, that is when he first overcomes you. Therefore, keep praising God, keep praying, and keep trusting God when you are in the midst of a battle.

Let me ask you a question: Are the battles in which you're engaged right now worth fighting, or are you just constantly defending yourself, upset, offended, and trying to prove how important you are? If they are worth the fight, go for it, and may God be with you. However, more likely than not, these skirmishes are causing you to waste good time and energy. I would dare to say that most of our battles and frustrations are petty and not worth the struggle. If they do not serve your divine destiny purpose, let go! Your Goliath conflict may arise and you will be too tired to fight the fight that truly matters, one whose reward can thrust you into your destiny.

When my son comes for a visit to my house, he occasionally will leave the light on in his room, ditch his shoes on the floor, or fall asleep with the television on. In the past I would nag him, but it would create unnecessary tension. Do I want him to do the responsible thing? Yes! But do I want us at odds during his infrequent visits? No! This battle doesn't have a big reward. This battle is not worth me losing my peace and causing our brief time to be stressful. I choose to let it go, although I might tell him his future wife may have an issue with it! We then laugh and move on. There may be other significant battles down the road that I will really need to fight with God's mighty help.

Spouses, what is the point of winning the argument just to be left in a silent stalemate with your spouse? Every marriage has issues and areas that need to be improved. However, some battles in our lives we bring upon ourselves, and then we complain "when it rains." But in situations of true discord, we have to look up to heaven and ask God for wisdom to best deal with it. It's easy to start a fight, but it can be hard to end a fight. I like what Proverbs 20:3 says, "It is honorable for a man to stop striving, since any fool can start a quarrel." Learn to keep the peace in your home and not argue about trivial or insignificant things. Be wise in what you choose to discuss (notice I said discuss, not quarrel here). We know that a bulldog can overcome a skunk any day of the week, but even a dog knows not to get involved with a skunk because it's not really worth the stink. You may be right, but is it really worth the stink, tension, and fuss?

It is usually the petty things in life that destroy the blossoming blessings that God has in store for us. Just like the proverbial grain of sand in our shoe, it's not really the major stuff but the minor stuff that can spoil a relationship, a business deal, a ministry, momentum, or your connection with God. The Word tells us in Song of Solomon 2:15, "Catch all the foxes, those little foxes, before they ruin the vineyard of love" (NLT). In other words, stop things that may create havoc and chaos, but don't fight battles you have no business fighting. Anything left unchecked can grow into something bigger that can cause much more damage later on. So, take care of what you have to take care of, and surrender what is out of your control to God.

Sometimes those "little foxes" are simply the case of good versus best. The battles surface because we have made small compromises of the flesh that are leading us to sin and ruin. A tactic of the enemy is to desensitize us and cause us to be involved in battles that will bring forth our destruction. Some people ask me, "Pastor, is there really a devil or enemy (his fallen angels and demonic oppression)?" Yes, the devil does exist. If there were no devil, why would God send His Son to fight what does not exist? The Bible says in 1 John 3:8, "He who sins is of the devil, for the devil has sinned from the beginning. For this purpose the Son of God was manifested, that He might destroy the works of the devil." The enemy tries to keep us passive toward the Word of God, causing us to lose focus, get stressed, and quit doing what is right. Don't let anyone or anything steal your joy and peace! Ask God for forgiveness and keep praising Him in your storm and sunshine.

The main battle that we have to fight is that of faith. This conflict actually exists between our ears, so to speak. Our corrupted world has a way of polluting our minds, which brings anxiety that causes us to compromise our Christian walk. We are on fire for the Lord one day and tepid the next. In the New Testament, the Apostle Paul encouraged his spiritual son, Timothy, to fight the good fight of faith. Why? Because negativity, doubt, and destructive thoughts have the tendency to creep in if we don't surrender our burdens to Christ. There is a saying, "You can't stop the birds from flying over your head, but you can certainly stop them from making a nest in your hair." It is the same way with these little negative thoughts that just nag us and come to us when least expected. That would be a little fox. You have to stop it right then and there by saying, "No. Get out of here in the name of Jesus."

Stress is another battle we don't need to fight. I know it feels like a big fox, but it's really a little one. In the Bible, Jesus instructs us to cast ALL our cares unto him. He also tells us to release our burdens unto Him, for His yoke is light. When we take matters into our own hands, we allow small issues to become big problems. How do you fight this particular little fox? You fight it God's way, not your way! Praise God out loud anyway, even though you do not truly feel it, and surrender this battle or burden unto Him. Another way to combat the little fox of stress is to look for the good in the situation. There will always be good if you look for it. Another way is to simply get quiet—just make yourself stop, center in, think about Jesus with your mind and in your heart, and look unto Him. Choose to get peaceful!

Sometimes a little fox can be something bad that is a constant discouragement, disappointment, or obstacle in your life. Fight, fight, fight to defeat it, but never ignore or run from it! You are an overcomer! God has equipped you with His DNA to be able to press through the mess. I know no one walks in the Spirit 24/7, but choose to walk in the Spirit as much as possible, which will help you do right and trust God!

Another little fox that is really dangerous is choosing the wrong friends, who can trap you with wrong influences. Our choice of friends can many times bring battles that were not in God's plan. Understand that when you come out of the world and you start following Jesus, most of the time your circle of friends will change. But trust that God will bring people into your life that will be better friends. You will encounter a fray of rejection and sometimes even persecution. Surrender this battle to Him and pray for those so-called friends that no longer want to be in your life. Know that the true friends that God will provide for you are friends who will be there for you through thick and thin. You don't ever want to let go of the friends that God wants you to hold on to and has appointed you with. I really love my friends (you know who you are)! I'm a blessed man because of them.

Some of us awoke today focusing on the "mountain" in our lives rather than on the living God who is higher than any mountain. Spiritual warfare emerges when you are doing the right thing and when you are about to experience a promotion. You must understand that your faith will carry you through! In some battles you will have to fight, but in this battle the Lord is saying, "The battle is Mine; do you trust Me?"

Maybe you are facing what seems like an impossible situation right now. You can't even see beyond the conflict. Simply position yourself to be strong in Christ by being ALL IN with His Word. Choose to praise and worship Him so your focus shifts from dwelling in the big problem to rising above it, thereby making it smaller. Trust blindly that God will fight your battle, because after all, He is your only constant. He's got this! The hotter the battle, the sweeter the victory! You may be knocked down, but you're not knocked out! Your blessing may have been delayed, but it has not been denied. You may have been held down, but speak to the devil like David spoke to Goliath and say, "Don't count me out, for God's not finished with me yet!"

You may be feeling weary in your endeavor to consistently do well. It may feel like you are getting pummeled, but God is doing some transformation where it counts—in your spiritual inward man. You may not be seeing it, but something's changing and something's moving. Focus on 2 Corinthians 4:16–18, which says, "Therefore we do not lose heart. Even though our outward man is perishing, yet the inward man is being renewed day by day. For our light affliction, which is but for a moment, is working for us a far more exceeding and eternal weight of glory, while we do not look at the things which are seen, but at the things which are not seen. For the things which are seen are temporary, but the things which are not seen are eternal." Don't procrastinate; right now, use one of the most powerful spiritual weapons available to you—your ability to praise Him! Praise Him who is not seen, for He and His ways are eternal.

When Jesus was crucified, many witnessed this horrendous, brutal death; but what they didn't see—because it was in the invisible realm—were the wonderful benefits this sacrifice allotted to mankind. If the dark rulers of this world would have known about those benefits, they would have never crucified Jesus. What was visible (the "seen") was His torment, torture, and brutal crucifixion death; but there was something bigger going on in the spiritual realm that would last for eternity. Glory!

Listen, I know it's challenging to focus on the spiritual things that have eternal implications when your teenager is acting up, your marriage is going south, the doctor says, "It doesn't look good; I need to do more tests," you get laid off, or your house payment is due and you have no money in the bank. But take heed: God says these things are not real. They do, however, stretch, pressure, and rake you over the hot coals. In other words, everything that you see (the visible and temporary) came out of the world you can't see (invisible and eternal). The Bible says to fix your eyes on the invisible (which is real as well as eternal). Don't get all agitated and bothered; know that the pressure you are enduring is purifying you into the human equivalent of 24-karat gold. Your inward man is being renewed.

It's safe to say that what is coming against you now is temporary. Trust that God will change it for glory (that which has always been, is, and cannot be changed). God is turning your temporary issue into a blessing that cannot be taken away from you. Hallelujah! What is seen comes and goes, but what is not seen stays! Just as a lightbulb when electrified emits light, or a car when fueled moves, God can take your problems, troubles, stress, and afflictions and turn them into glory. What you're going through shall come to pass, but what you're going to get shall never fade.

Do you ever wonder what would happen if you took your eyes off of your battles for a week and just concentrated on giving God praise, love, and worship by praying, fasting, and focusing on things that have an eternal connection? Great things, I venture! Don't give up, my friend. Focus on His plan, His way, and His will for your life. Take your eyes off the preacher, spouse, or whomever else is distracting you and fix your eyes on the Great I Am, who will never let you down. You will not be disappointed nor will you regret it.

Can you trust Him? You will either quit or continue based on your focus! A dog on the hunt doesn't know it has fleas. When you are in hot pursuit of something, you don't allow petty annoyances to distract you from your goal. If you are complaining, gossiping, murmuring, and noticing the fleas, it's only because you don't have sufficient focus on your vision, goal, or the great and mighty delivering God you serve.

I want to leave you with seven ways you can position yourself better and have tenacious focus in your earthly battles.

How to Position Yourself So That God Fights Your Battle

1. Surrender the battle to God, allowing His vengeance to be done

It's time you know your authority in Christ Jesus. God has given you dominion so you won't waste time on battles that are meaningless or not attainable. One of the best things you can do for yourself is to realize that the battle is not yours and that we all have limitations. Acknowledge that you need to completely depend on God and His power, not yours. Zechariah 4:6 tells us that "Not by might, nor by power, but by My Spirit, says the Lord of hosts." God has the ultimate battle plan, but we insist on our own warfare and then ask God to bless it. That's not going to happen! Put it into the Master's hands.

2. Get serious and seek the Lord (prayer, reading, and quiet time alone)

We are in a spiritual fight, and we don't fight spiritual fights with natural weapons. We fight with faith and trust. Ask God for help! No need to stay in the dark wondering or worrying. Ephesians 6:17 says, "And take the helmet of salvation, and the sword of the Spirit, which is the word of God." The Word of God, our faith, and our words (worship and faith declarations) are our most effective weapons. Psalm 27:4–5 tells us to seek the Lord. I want to challenge you to have a made-up mind-set and to know that God's Word becomes a sword when you speak it in faith.

3. Worship (praise and sing) His mighty name
Why is this so important? Here are three solid reasons why:

1. Worship brings His presence. God goes where He is welcomed. He doesn't go where He is tolerated, but where He is celebrated. He is everywhere, but He manifests Himself where He is rejoiced and welcomed. Many people go to church but don't get the full benefits that come by truly worshipping Him. Church only benefits you when you genuinely celebrate His presence with praise and worship!

2. It makes you more like Christ, because you're entering a heavenly atmosphere and embracing His image. In life, your goal is to be "like Christ," not "like Mike." When you are in Christ, you do His bidding. Live doing the Word!

3. It puts your problems in a different perspective. You now see your problems from above (elevated view) instead of straight on (parallel view). You will see above and beyond any current sickness, money concerns, family issues, and so forth. Take your sights off your problems and put them on God. When your eyes are on God, all of a sudden your problems become small.

4. REMEMBER HIS PROMISES AND PAST VICTORIES

Refuse to give up unless God closes the door very tightly. There is a verse that always brings me peace no matter the chaos going on around me. It's found in Psalm 23:4: "Even though I walk through the valley of the shadow of death, I will fear no evil, for you are with me; your rod and your staff, they comfort me" (ESV).

5. MAKE THE TIME TO FAST

When the great multitudes of Moab and Ammon came against Judah, King Jehoshaphat proclaimed a fast throughout all of Judah. God didn't equip them with swords to fight their battle, but rather He honored their praises and fasting mind-set and ultimately granted them victory. In some battles, you can just cry out the name of Jesus and the victory is yours, but in others you will have to push through with a fast. Matthew 17:21 says, "But this kind [tougher battle] does not go out except by prayer and fasting" (NASB).

6. POSITION YOURSELF (STANDING STILL AND TRUSTING GOD DO THE WORK)

There are some battles that don't require you to fight; you can just show up trusting fully in God and enjoy the triumph. Learn how to pick the battles that are worth the struggle. Learn how to be still in the middle of a storm, trusting in the Great I Am. Learn to immediately default to prayer, thanking God that He is with you, rather than fretting and allowing anxiety to grow.

You know, if we were able to look at difficult—or better yet, wicked—people with the ability to see what drives them rather than only seeing them on the surface, we would have greater understanding and consideration. We also would not be as perplexed as to how to treat them, but we would be able to love them right where they are. We would see them with eyes of love and compassion and understand that they have simply become puppets in the hands of their puppet master, who is actually the enemy of their soul. Ephesians 6:12 says, "For we do not wrestle against flesh and blood, but against the rulers, against the authorities, against the cosmic powers over this present darkness, against the spiritual forces of evil in the heavenly places" (ESV). Soldier of the Lord, get in your battle position and trust your platoon commander's (Jesus Christ) Kingdom way of living!

7. COMMIT TO THE PLAN

There is a difference between interest (convenient) and commitment (no excuses, only results). Psalm 37:5 says, "Commit your way to the LORD; trust in him, and he will act" (ESV). Understand that commitment is the bridge to what you know and what you do! Many won't commit to your vision, but you must press on anyway—especially if it's a God-ordained Kingdom agenda vision. Some won't like you or agree with you. So what? Press through anyway! If God's got you, it's really no big deal if others don't. You should not waste your time and energy trying to change their minds or living in a certain way in order to prove something to them. You don't need anyone's approval to be who God made you to be. There are many roads that lead to success, but one sure road to failure is the road of trying to please everybody. If I had to guess, I would say the following of people you meet throughout your life:

- 25 percent won't like you
- 25 percent can be persuaded to like you
- 25 percent like you, but can have a fall out with you
- 25 percent like you no matter what

In conclusion, the best way to answer your critics is not with words but with actions. Let them see the fruit of a well-lived life. Let them see someone who is not afraid to live ALL IN for their Savior and Lord Jesus Christ.

14

SWEET SURRENDER

The mind governed by the flesh is hostile to God; it
does not submit to God's law, nor can it do so. Those
who are in the realm of the flesh cannot please God.

—ROMANS 8:7–8, NIV

A T SOME POINT in your life, someone will do
something to offend or disrespect you. If you've
never experienced this, just keep on living. We
can't always control what happens to us, but we do have
the ability to control how we respond. I personally used
to be a very vindictive person if someone would cross
me. This gradually caused me to become mean-spirited,
stressed, and angry. Rather than living "chillin," I was
very uptight. In Romans 12:19 Paul tells us, "Do not take
revenge, my dear friends, but leave room for God's wrath,
for it is written: 'It is mine to avenge; I will repay,' says
the Lord" (NIV). I have learned that the best revenge is my
joy in Christ, because nothing drives people crazier than
seeing someone actually enjoying a good life.

When I changed my mind-set from vindication to
surrender, my peace and joy returned. When I made it a
point to pray for those who would do or speak evil, my

peace and joy increased. When I made it a point to treat my accusers well despite them expecting me to attack, my peace and joy were sustained. When I would love them despite them treating me wrong, my peace and joy remained. I didn't have to fellowship with them, but I did have to love them, because that is the ultimate mark of a real Christian. In other words, I had to surrender myself to His will, plan, and Kingdom protocol.

I don't know about you, but I desire to have all the blessings that God has in store for me, my family, and the ministry that He has entrusted to me. First Peter 3:9 says, "not returning evil for evil or reviling for reviling, but on the contrary blessing, knowing that you were called to this, that you may inherit a blessing." If you are really a child of God, you have to give God the opportunity to vindicate you. Nothing escapes His eyes! We must continue to model Christ by being Christlike. You must not allow anything or anyone to steal your peace. A big price was paid for your peace, but you must sweetly surrender it all to God and resist your flesh to maintain it. Getting even isn't going to cut it! You don't need to carry that heavy burden, live with all that anxiety, or even try to understand the whole situation. Simply surrender it to the Great I Am and rest.

Jesus Christ the man prepares us for heaven, but the Word of God prepares us for earth. God wants you to have "heaven on earth" and live with dominion, not ulcers and resentment. You are saved—stop putting so much pressure on yourself because you keep falling short of perfection. However, you will not have heaven on earth, kingdom rights, fullness of blessings, and divine purpose being manifested if you choose to get even with people and live outside His will, His plan, and His way. If you don't surrender and trust God, you will live a life of constant stress—one of the leading causes of death in our society. However, if you are a child of God (not just a creation of God), take heed and be encouraged by the fact that people and conditions are limited in their ability to harm you.

Though we do have to be astute and cautious with wicked people and dangerous things that can injure us or even kill the body, the fact of the matter is, they can't touch the spirit/soul (the part that lives forever). Matthew 10:28 says, "And do not fear those who kill the body but cannot kill the soul. But rather fear Him who is able to destroy both soul and body in hell." The fact of the matter is, "if" you are certain of your eternity in heaven, you will or you should lose all of your earthly fears. I love this Bible verse, 2 Timothy 1:7: "For God has not given us a spirit of fear, but of power and of love and of a sound mind."

This doesn't mean we won't experience fear; it simply means we won't be controlled by it. The Bible also gives us the assurance in 2 Corinthians 5:8 that "We are confident, yes, well pleased rather to be absent from the body and to be present with the Lord." This is why I personally live fearlessly, because to me heaven is my homecoming! I am in this world but not of this world. Therefore, my friend, RiseUp and choose to surrender so that you will no longer live in fear. God will not commit to you till you submit to Him. I have held many things in my hands, and I have lost them all; but whatever I have placed in God's hands, those I still possess. God loves when we surrender and trust Him!

Here are seven examples of surrendering even further to God Almighty. This is where the rubber meets the road, folks. This is where we make Jesus not just our Savior, but our Lord. This is basically where we go from self-living to Christ-living.

Examples of Surrendering

Surrendering to Jesus Christ is another name for "being born again."

We are all born with a "dead" spirit that we need to bring to life by launching a connection with God through His Son, Jesus Christ. Not much will make sense unless that is first established. The Holy Spirit will take ownership and guide you to all truth thereafter, but you must surrender to His lordship first.

Surrendering is allowing Jesus Christ to live inside you and entrusting Him with all your decisions.

This goes a step deeper in that you will acknowledge Him in all your ways. It's making Him not just your Savior, but your Lord of all.

Surrendering means living a godly life that is pleasing and acceptable to Jesus.

There are two guarantees in life: death and God's 100 percent-guaranteed promises. Live for Him, because the alternative will never bring you the satisfaction that your soul craves.

Surrendering is confessing and repenting your sins.

This means turning away from and not continuing to live with a deliberately sinful lifestyle. It's rather scary living so routinely in sin that you don't see the need to repent from it. Understand that you cannot rebuke a devil to whom you continuously grant access to your life. Many Christians are living in bondage, captivity, and entanglement because they habitually keep sinning without repenting. They are in dire straits and truly need to repent! The evidence of true repentance is gradual, or in some cases, immediate transformation; definitely not staying the same or living in shackles. Too many people are living without the fear of the Lord and therefore continue to live in repetitious sinning without even a desire to change. Change is not change until there is genuine transformation.

Salvation is not the final destination on earth. If we are stuck in a sin or an addiction that has us entangled, we have to do our part, which is to fight and allow God to do His part in the spiritual realm. This is part of the blessing that our relational God offers us in this "creation with Creator" rapport. Rest easy in the fact that He will not give you more than you can handle, which simply means you are equipped to pass your current test or trial and break free of the sin that has you chained. Freedom is yours, but it won't come easy. You will have to surrender, resist, and break through, all empowered by His strength. The resisting part will be the most challenging. You will have to sweat and depend on His strength. I'm convinced that a believer who lives in willful disobedience to God cannot experience the delight that obedience brings.

SURRENDERING MEANS GIVING UP PRIDE, INDEPENDENCE, AND CONTROL.

Don't enter the boxing ring of satanic activity alone in your own strength. Understand and rest in the fact that the battle is already won and all you really have to do is fight for your mind.

SURRENDERING ALLOWS YOU TO ACCEPT THE FREE GIFT OF GRACE.

Surrendering and accepting this free gift empowers you. But keep in mind that grace doesn't mean you can now sin freely; let it change you.

SURRENDERING IS THE ONE THING THAT WILL ALLOW YOU TO HAVE ETERNAL LIFE IN HEAVEN AND A HAPPIER LIFE HERE ON EARTH.

Many theologies promise some semblance of heaven, but not necessarily heaven on earth. Fight for your mind so you can have both! When you are truly saved by His gift of grace, you want to live for Him. Eternity is too costly, not to mention permanent, to play around with it. You can't please God while living for self. You will abide forever in either heaven or in hell, depending on whom you live for here on earth. I pray for God's continued grace and mercy on those who choose to gamble with God.

Life is a struggle, but there are some struggles and burdens we just don't need to carry. I have no doubt that your best days are ahead of you and not behind you if you keep surrendering and staying broken to the Potter, allowing Him to continue molding you into His Son's likeness. Paradoxically, you are not very useful until you are broken! Bread had to be broken to feed the five thousand, the sinful woman had to break the seal of her alabaster box to release that expensive perfume, and Jesus's body had to be broken in order to bring us salvation. Sometimes it takes a person to be completely empty, destitute, and at their wits' end to be able to be filled by God. Stop trying to change others, and take a hard look at yourself. In other words, take your hand off the remote that changes the channel of your spouse, child, parents, siblings, or friends and hand it back to the Creator. You know when we lose something or surrender to something godly, we always gain something better.

To whom are you going to surrender—yourself or God? Just know for a fact that the safest place to be in the entire universe is in the will of God! Grow in your faith and spiritual maturity, keep surrendering, and press through the mess. You don't need to carry all that baggage; life can be lighter and more manageable. Have you ever heard someone say, "Oh, those were my glory days," when reflecting on their past? I'm convinced that people who believe their best days are behind them are rarely prosperous in their finances, personal growth, or relationships, not to mention they often struggle with unhappiness and depression. Believe and declare that the best is still yet to come as you enjoy your present!

The Christian life is not as hard as we try to make it; it's really a battle of the mind, not necessarily a battle with demons. The Word doesn't say "hold demons captive," but "hold thoughts captive." But some take advice and others crash. Some choose to remain in bondage while others fight for their internal freedom. Free yourself today, in Jesus's name, by surrendering to His mighty power! Instead of detaching yourself from the problem, attach yourself to God's promises. If you are stuck in a habit or addiction, surrender your will and replace it with prayer, fasting, and determination (resistance). Sometimes you have to experience severe deprivation in order to receive celebration. Sometimes God allows you to get to the very bottom of the well, so to speak, so you can look up and put your whole dependence on Him for a change. I pray for God's people to walk in complete and total surrender so they can receive God's ultimate.

His will for your life has been set. Whatever you're thinking about, He's already on it, because He knows your thoughts before your thoughts become your own. Did you get that? Read it again and allow it to really soak in. Recognize that He already knows what He is going to do, and whatever that may be, it is exceedingly and abundantly above all that you have and can ask of Him. Stop chasing your feelings and begin chasing your God. Feelings do not merit obedience and surrender. Repentance, not remorse, is what you need!

Surrender the thing that holds you down and cease worrying about it. Don't spend another sleepless night concerned about it; don't ask another person or look for another sanction about it. God has a plan for you, and His ways are higher than anything that is against you! Give it to God and rest. Some things in life are beyond our control. It is the wise person who has the ability to surrender and stop carrying the weight of anything about which God has already said, "The battle is over!" The storms of life affect us all, but the person who anchors his or her soul on God has security in the midst of any tempest. There is no need to fear or worry, for the Holy Spirit will lead you—if you let Him.

Jesus succeeded in his earthy mission because He surrendered to His Father's will rather than His own. Understand that when your rights to yourself (your will) are surrendered to God, your true personal nature immediately begins responding to God. Freedom, peace, and complete victory through Jesus Christ come into your life, causing you to gradually transform into His likeness. I have done the most growing and received the most blessings (albeit not necessarily material ones) when I have surrendered whatever I was battling. Whatever that "it" may be for you, let it go from your hands into God's hands. Say, "God, I don't need to understand it, I don't need to know when or why; I just need to trust You, Lord! Your perfect will shall be done here on earth as it is in heaven. I choose today to live ALL IN for you!"

15

TENACIOUSLY AND WHOLEHEARTEDLY TRUSTING GOD

The LORD is my rock and my fortress and my
deliverer; my God, my strength, in whom I will trust;
my shield and the horn of my salvation, my stronghold.
—PSALM 18:2

I S THE LORD truly your Shepherd? How can some of
you reply that He is, if when life trips you up, you
easily panic? We all have chaotic moments that bring
fear, but if you really know who your anchor, refuge, and
rock is, there will be more serenity than panic. Trusting
in God and being filled with His Holy Spirit will open
the door—actually, more like the floodgates—for us to
be filled with hope (true expectation), joy (internal and
external gladness), and peace (friendship with God,
internal peace, spiritual relaxation). This is certainly a
promise to cling to! A therapist, counselor, psychologist,
psychiatrist, social worker, or life coach cannot compare
to this. I have nothing against these professionals, but
I would rather put all of my trust in the Author and
Finisher of my faith.

Timing plays an important part in learning to trust God. Some of us act and pray like He's a genie in a bottle—when trouble and trials creep up on us, we call out for His help. We complain and murmur when the answer doesn't come in our expected timing. We don't go to church consistently, we don't serve Him, and we don't seek Him, yet we complain when things don't go as we have planned. We want God to answer our prayer petition as soon as possible. If God were to quickly answer our prayers and do everything we asked for immediately, we would never grow and develop the character to trust in Him! Are you sure you know God? Because if you did, you would know that most of His answered prayers are not immediately answered. You see, if you knew Him, you would trust in His timing.

The most precious thing to God about you is not your IQ, monetary offerings, or musical talent. The most precious thing to God is your trust in Him. The same God that stood beside Daniel in the lion's den is standing right beside you in your present troubled scenario. God told Moses, "You do the little thing of extending your rod to the Red Sea and I will do the big thing of opening it up so that My people [the Israelites], will be able to walk on dry land." Moses probably thought God was going to have him do something big, but the great thing he had to do was simply put his trust in the Great I Am.

Being still can be especially challenging when your subconscious is nagging you with questions such as "Now what are you going to do?" Know that peace comes to those who still hope even though they've been disappointed, to those who still believe though they've been betrayed, to those who still love even though they've been hurt, and to those who still trust in God though He is momentarily silent. When God is involved, anything can happen. Our job is to trust Him because He has a beautiful way of bringing good out of crisis and broken situations. Man says, "Show me and I'll trust you," but God says, "Trust Me and I'll show you!"

Don't fear that you will seem foolish when you choose to follow the Lord—He guides and comforts, and you will never be steered wrong by trusting in Him. Stop fearing and start trusting, because His leadership will be your defense. His track record and promises are proven. Follow His way and live with complete peace. Let God lead you to the still waters that refresh your soul. Let Him be your guide. Allow Him to instruct and lead you, for He cares so much for you. Let His Spirit be your best counsel, because He will provide the right answer each time. Let Him fight your battle, because His will always be the best outcome. Whatever you decide to do, just make sure you trust Him.

Learn to trust in Him and listen to His voice without trying to figure it all out yourself. Confirmation will soon come! Take your mind out of the equation. You don't have to "get it" or "understand it," but you do have to trust in Him to make it right! The Bible never once says, "figure it out," but over and over tells us to "trust God." He's already got it all figured out. Some people may disagree with you, but understand that God never commanded you to trust people. He commanded you to love people and trust Him. Know the difference. Your joy and victory depend on it.

It's Monday and you just don't "feel it" today. You slump around, wondering what your future holds. I have three words for you: "Trust your Maker." You broke up with your boyfriend or girlfriend, and you're anxious because your time clock is ticking and you want to get married. Same three words: "Trust your Maker." You and your teenager are having major communication issues. What do you do? You pray, love them unconditionally exactly where they're at, don't take things personally, and "Trust your Maker." You've lost some of that "loving feeling" toward your spouse and you're contemplating divorce. What to do now? You look for the good that your spouse brings to the relationship, you understand life is but a vapor, and you "Trust your Maker" to heal your heart while you do what the Word in Ephesians commands us to do regarding our spouse. You're concerned because your life has no excitement and nothing is happening. What do you do? You "Trust your Maker," because great things happen in silence. Each day the sun sends its powerful rays over all the earth without making a single sound. You should never say "Yes, God" or "I Trust You, God" and be ashamed, regardless of your past. You simply cannot go wrong by trusting in Him!

I recently spoke to an elderly pastor regarding his sixty-three-year marriage which has yielded six children and eighteen grandchildren. He spoke so beautifully about his wife while I was just trying to wrap my mind around how being married for sixty-three years is even possible. My mind just couldn't grasp it! He was totally transparent with me, and I hung on to every word he said. He went on to mention that there had been many times when he wanted out and times when she did as well. He recounted how sometimes the heated arguments were so intense, they wouldn't even kiss goodnight. He declared that even though he loves his wife, marriage is challenging and for the mature partaker, not the faint of heart.

During our conversation, I made the following request: "Pastor, I'm divorced and recently remarried. Please give me three tips on the secret to the success of your marriage."

While he pondered the question, my mind was anxiously anticipating his answer. I began to make guesses in my mind—"Oh, he's probably going to say a good friendship, lots of love, patience, respect, or something to that effect."

He kept mulling it over while staring out into the distance and then finally said to me, "Are you ready for the answer?"

I replied, "Bring it, Sir!"

He then gazed intently into my eyes and said, "Trust God, trust God, trust God."

I was speechless! I was so astounded by his answer that I blurted out, "That's it?" to which he replied, "That's all you really need." The advice this sage gave me that day has been anchored to my soul ever since. I love my wife, Sandra, but like all couples in the process of becoming one flesh, we have our challenges. Whenever I feel frustrated because we are not achieving certain goals as quickly as I would like, I repeat the words that wise man of God shared with me that day: "Trust God, trust God, trust God."

TRUSTING GOD, NOT OURSELVES

Humanly speaking, it might be prudent to have confidence in your own abilities. Humanly speaking, when you cannot trust anyone around you, you must trust in yourself. I have heard many people say over and over, "I only trust myself. I don't trust anyone else!" The Book of Proverbs 3:5–7 says, "Trust in the LORD with all your heart and lean not on your own understanding; in all your ways submit to him, and he will make your paths straight. Do not be wise in your own eyes; fear the LORD and shun evil."

This passage has been an anchor in my life, especially whenever I have been tempted to do things without God's input. I've read it a thousand times, and it keeps me focused on what I need to do. I've come to the conclusion that the safest place in the whole wide world is being and staying in the will of God! Therefore, my goal is to conquer each day with a powerful morning prayer and a mind-set that my trust will be completely in Him.

It's far easier to have faith in God than not to. There are even unbelievers who have their own version of faith in God. However, even though having faith in God can be relatively easy, it's a lot harder to exercise trust in Him. Have you noticed in many situations that as long as things are under control, all is well? It's only when crises erupt that life becomes a mess! I've noticed that as long as there is no opposition, people are basically content, but when they are pushed, they panic. Where is God when all hell breaks loose? Exactly where He was when you were on the mountaintop. Trusting God does not require any sweat or tears—only submission to God and resistance of the devil. If nothing in your life makes sense right now, trust God blindly nonetheless! Many of us are so far down in the valley that we really won't have much to lose anyway.

In the Bible, there is a story about a man named Job who endured possibly the greatest challenges a person could go through. It's difficult to imagine ever having it as bad as Job, and it's unlikely we ever will suffer his trials. Job was a righteous and wealthy family man. However, he lost his ten children, his cattle, his wealth, and his friends, he got a nasty skin disease, and to top it off, he had a nagging wife who wanted him to curse God.

This man, who at one point had it all, went through one of the most horrific series of ordeals in history. His very name is associated with hardships and difficulties! Perhaps you see yourself in a very challenging situation today where the things you were counting on have disappeared, or even the ground you were standing on has slipped out from under you. Your faith has sunk low or has been shattered because of devastating disappointments. Everything you had planned seems meaningless now. I would like to encourage you to be patient in your valley and declare what the prophet Job said: "Though He slay me, yet will I trust Him" (Job 13:15). How can a loving God who abides by His promises not honor this mind-set? You can trust God completely without completely understanding Him. God will never call you to a place where He is not already present. Press through your mess and say today, "Lord, I trust You no matter what!"

SIX REASONS WHY TRUST SHOULD BE A PRIORITY FOR CHRISTIANS

1. IT RELATES DIRECTLY TO GOD'S CHARACTER

When you distrust, it implies God is unreliable.

2. IT HELPS US TO REMEMBER HIS PROMISES AND TO CONFESS THEM (REJOICE AND DON'T COMPLAIN)

Psalm 145:13 says, "Your kingdom is an everlasting kingdom, and Your dominion endures throughout all generations."

There is something about a promise from God that will secure your soul, comfort your heart, and bring peace to your mind. When nothing else works, His Word still does. Be it praise or protest, whatever flows from your lips will affect your life!

3. IT HELPS US DEPEND ON GOD, KNOWING HE IS ALWAYS THERE

Hebrews 13:5 says, "Let your conduct be without covetousness; be content with such things as you have. For He Himself has said, "I will never leave you nor forsake you."

4. IT IGNITES OUR SOUL TO BUCKLE UP

Psalm 91:2 says, "I will say of the LORD, 'He is my refuge and my fortress; my God, in Him I will trust.'"

Don't ever attempt to weather a storm or a valley without God.

5. HE WANTS YOU TO SHINE HIS LIGHT TO ALL MANKIND

Jesus didn't save you just so you can make it to heaven. He suffered death on the cross for you so that you would be able to walk in the image of His Father. He wants you to live in abundance here on earth replete with joy, peace, fulfillment, health, prosperity, and freedom. Choose to be ALL IN by letting your light shine for the entire world to see.

6. TO FULLY SURRENDER AND OBEY IMPACTS THE SOUL AND BRINGS FULLNESS OF BLESSINGS

A perfect example of this is when Jesus Himself trusted His heavenly Father's will over His own. Another illustration is when Mary put her trust in God and His message that her baby would be the Savior of the world despite her fiancé doubting her word, having to give birth in a manger among animals, and Herod hunting the Christ child down.

Sadly, many Christians believe in a God they do not trust. Have you at times questioned the rationale for this disconnect? I believe the reason is because many possess faith to get themselves to heaven but lack trust in a God who will help them navigate through life here and now. God will interrupt your plans sometimes just as He did with Mary when she was about to marry Joseph. Can you still trust Him? Yes! In fact, it is when He disrupts your carefully set out strategies that you truly can and must trust Him. You see, when you fully trust God, He will give you the capacity to see things completely finished despite the present noise, attitudes, and resistance.

The presence of fear does not have to mean the absence of faith; you can still trust Him. Perhaps you are saying, "I'm just too frustrated to trust in anybody or anything!" Don't lose hope because you have frustrations. Remember, even Mary was frustrated when she was chosen to deliver our Savior. Being frustrated does not mean you don't have favor. In fact, you can be powerful and still be in pain! Can you trust Him anyway? Yes! God will make something beautiful of your life, but He needs your trust in Him to do it. Your job—or "your mission, should you choose to accept it"—is to simply trust Him.

We also have to choose to trust God in our romantic relationships. Many people have a greater fear of living alone than a desire to live right. Instead of pleasing the One who created, formed, and planned you, who gave you plans and a purpose, not to mention gave you salvation and has promised you heaven, we choose to trust in our feelings for another person. You can't be living together prior to marriage, fornicating, and expect God to fully bless your relationship. The wages of sin brings death of some type, especially a loss in the passion to chase after God's presence. How can you expect God to answer your prayers or bless your mess when you are living wrong and out of sync with His will? That's like calling the police to arrest somebody for stealing your homegrown weed.

We try to grasp God's unlimited ways of doing things with our limited mind. If things don't happen in the time we allot, we falsely think that it's not to be and we back out from persistent prayers, church attendance, and chasing after His heart with passion. Some of His plans and ways won't be understood until we get to heaven. His vision supersedes our nearsighted requests that are focused on the thirst of the day and not the droughts of the future.

When God does something we don't understand, we have a tendency to want to back out. Don't let this happen to you! Life is designed to test your staying power. Do all that you can to stand when you don't understand. The key is to stay consistent and grounded, and to continue putting your trust in God even when life gets complicated or an unexpected scenario unfolds.

There are also many people who live in poverty or financial stress because they fail to trust in Jehovah Jireh, our provider. Because they lack faith that God will provide, they are stingy with their giving. What they don't comprehend is that they can't outgive God. We know according to Scripture in Philippians 4:19 that He will supply all of our needs, yet they continue to live in fear and doubt His Word. They'll go to dinner and spend $50 on a meal, but they won't sow a $5 seed to a kingdom ministry. For the record, we must understand that everything starts with a seed. A seed knows its assignment. Seeds receive invisible instructions from God, who is the Lord of the harvest. A harvest yields only what the voice of the seed instructs. Every good and abundant harvest comes from God, and He does it all through a seed. So, have faith, trust God, sow a seed, and expect the increase!

Before I go deeper into the benefits of tenaciously trusting in the Great I Am, I want to convey the importance of fixing our eyes on the things of the kingdom, the things not seen. The Bible instructs us to focus on them and not on things which are seen, for those things are only temporary. There is more above our heads than below our feet. What you see, touch, hear, smell, or taste is temporary, but the things you cannot see will transform you.

If Satan can keep you looking at the temporary, then he can keep you focused on something that was simply meant to pass by. The kingdom is seen with the mind, and the enemy of our souls blinds the mind. He blinds you to eternal things by keeping you focused on temporary things. In other words, if he can keep you focused on your troubles (illness, toxic relationship, etc.), he can keep you from perceiving your quality future.

TEN BENEFITS OF TENACIOUSLY TRUSTING IN GOD

1. GIVES YOU DELIVERANCE

> Our fathers trusted in You; they trusted, and You delivered them. They cried to You, and were delivered; they trusted in You, and were not ashamed.
>
> —PSALM 22:4–5

2. BLESSES YOU

> Blessed is that man who makes the LORD his trust, and does not respect the proud, nor such as turn aside to lies.
>
> —PSALM 40:4

3. GIVES YOU HOPE

> For You are my hope, O Lord GOD; You are my trust from my youth.
>
> —PSALM 71:5

4. GIVES YOU SELF-CONFIDENCE

It is better to trust in the Lord than to put confidence in man.

—PSALM 118:8

5. GIVES YOU PEACE

You will keep him in perfect peace, whose mind is stayed on You, because he trusts in You.

—ISAIAH 26:3

6. GIVES YOU COURAGE

Therefore thus says the Lord God: "Behold, I lay in Zion a stone for a foundation, a tried stone, a precious cornerstone, a sure foundation; whoever believes will not act hastily."

—ISAIAH 28:16

7. GIVES YOU STRENGTH

For thus says the Lord God, the Holy One of Israel: "In returning and rest you shall be saved; in quietness and confidence shall be your strength." But you would not.

—ISAIAH 30:15

8. GIVES YOU A FOUNDATION TO GROW ON

Thus says the Lord: "Cursed is the man who trusts in man and makes flesh his strength, whose heart departs from the Lord.... Blessed is the man who trusts in the Lord, and whose hope is the Lord. For he shall be like a tree planted by the waters, which spreads out its roots by the river, and

will not fear when heat comes; but its leaf will
be green, and will not be anxious in the year of
drought, nor will cease from yielding fruit."

—JEREMIAH 17:5, 7–8

9. IT CALMS YOUR WORRIES, AND RELIEVES YOUR ACHING HEART AND ANXIOUS SOUL

Let not your heart be troubled; you believe in
God, believe also in Me.

—JOHN 14:1

10. ALLOWS YOU TO FREE YOUR MIND FROM THE INABILITY TO UNDERSTAND HIM

"For My thoughts are not your thoughts,
nor are your ways My ways," says the Lord.
"For as the heavens are higher than the earth,
so are My ways higher than your ways, and My
thoughts than your thoughts."

—ISAIAH 55:8–9

As this chapter comes to a close, I want to ask you if
you are feeling frustrated and are mentally struggling
because your life is not going the way you anticipated. In
other words, you pray, go to church, and read your Bible,
yet nothing is happening in your favor. You ask yourself,
"What's wrong with me?" That's where we mess up. We
want to trust in anyone or anything other than the Lord.
We will trust in our own abilities, our boss's judgment,
our money, our doctor, and even in an airline pilot. But
the Lord, well...

It's easy to trust in things we can see. Sure, we believe in
God, but to allow Him to run our life? That's asking a little
too much; after all, don't we have free will? Advertising
and peer pressure blind us with the world's view of what

is important: a high-paying career, a head-turning car, a gorgeous home, and a spouse or significant other who will make everyone else around us green with envy. These are things you can see and enjoy now, but will they last?

What is the best way to trust? Allow the guidance of the Holy Spirit to take precedence. He knows what's right, wrong, and who or what is connected to your destiny. I know it's scary and might cause you to proceed forward with hesitancy, but proceed you must. And the strength to advance comes from trusting God to lead the way.

Trusting in the Lord tenaciously may even require you to abandon everything you've ever believed in and depended on. However, you can rest in the fact that God will make something beautiful of your life—but He needs your trust in Him to do it. Therefore, delight in the Lord, trust in His plan, and rest in Him. But don't be fooled—resting may sound easy, but it requires supernatural courage, because it is our human tendency to fret. Worry turns our minds away from delighting and trusting in the Lord. Patiently waiting is a supreme test of our spiritual maturity. Are you ready? The time to start is today, right now. It's time to RiseUp and be ALL IN for God, who will require us to put our trust in things we do not see![1]

16

EMBRACING THE FIRE
OF THE HOLY SPIRIT

I indeed baptize you with water unto repentance,
but He who is coming after me is mightier than
I, whose sandals I am not worthy to carry. He
will baptize you with the Holy Spirit and fire.

—MATTHEW 3:11

HUMANS WERE NOT created to depend solely on
their own strength. We were created to be power-assisted. We were made for the fire of the Holy
Spirit. Salvation is not the climax of Christianity on this
earth. Before Jesus ascended to heaven, He left us a gift to
help us here and now. The Holy Spirit is a gift from the
Father, much like your salvation is a gift. He has given the
Holy Spirit to you to draw you closer to Him into a more
intimate relationship. In this chapter, I will elaborate and
we will go a little deeper into this person of the Trinity.

When you receive the gift of salvation, your earthly
spirit is "born again," connecting you with God, who is
not a human but a Spirit. The next step is for your body
to be baptized in water, an outward symbol of an inward

transformation.[1] But God also desires for your soul to get baptized in the Spirit. He wants a consuming fire to embrace you so you can live with exceptional boldness for His glory. Many of the disciples were doubters and cowards prior to receiving the baptism of the Holy Spirit in their souls on the Day of Pentecost. The Holy Spirit, our Helper or Counselor whom Jesus left us, empowers us like power steering does a car so we are able to do things we cannot do in our own strength.

We need the Spirit's help to resist the enemy, crucify our own flesh, and live with boldness and power. The reason why so many Christians powerlessly stumble around with no direction, boldness, or purpose is because they are walking without the Spirit—they are doing life in their own limited strength. Many are ashamed to even preach the gospel or invite people to church, because that bold confidence has not set in. We need this Helper (what can be called Holy Spirit fire) in our lives so we will be able to share the gospel just like we would promote a good movie. The fire of the Holy Spirit will ignite a passion and boldness for Christ that will strengthen weak spines. God's Word wants you to embrace that fire as it says in Luke 12:49 (ESV), "I came to cast fire on the earth, and would that it were already kindled!"

Jesus lived a very powerful, impactful, and amazing life, yet for all the miracles He performed, He said that we (you and I) would do even greater things. I believe it wholeheartedly! He was born of the Spirit, baptized by the Spirit, anointed with the Spirit, and resurrected through the Spirit. Thus, His Spirit has power! It's the same Spirit that raised Lazarus from the dead, and this same Spirit is now available to those who don't doubt and simply choose to embrace it. Many churches in America shy away from inviting the fullness of the Spirit to dwell among them. I am convinced that the less of the Holy Spirit we have in church, the more entertainment we will need to keep the church going. God wants His fire to spread!

When Jesus gave the Great Commission (Matt. 28:16–20), He knew that His disciples could not fulfill it in their own power; therefore, He had a special gift in store for them. It was His plan to give them the same firepower that He had. On the Day of Pentecost, all 120 people who were present in the Upper Room received the flame of the Holy Spirit. Unfortunately, there were about another 400 that should have been there but for whatever reason failed to attend. Others didn't receive it because they doubted or did not follow what Jesus had instructed. Divine power was to be given according to Acts 1:8, "But you shall receive power when the Holy Spirit has come upon you; and you shall be witnesses to Me in Jerusalem, and in all Judea and Samaria, and to the end of the earth." Holy Spirit power was available to all, but most chose to trust, live, and operate in their own limited ability. That sad decision continues to be made today.

Are you a blood-washed Christian? In other words, are you saved by His grace? If your answer is yes, then you qualify for this power. That's all you need to do; simply accept His gift of salvation. Now, for those of you who are being tormented by feelings of guilt, unworthiness, and condemnation because you can't get this "Christ walk" right, I have good news for you: it comes to the best and worst of us! God sees your struggles, He sees your failings, and He sees your weaknesses, but by His grace you are made strong in your weakness.

You can't earn this Holy Spirit fire that comes from God Almighty. The Bible says in Hebrews 12:29, "For our God is a consuming fire." If God wants you to have it, what's stopping you from getting it? The way the Spirit works in our lives is a mystery, but understand that what you don't know, your spirit already knows. This is why you sometimes feel frustrated because you know you have a future but your mind can't comprehend what it is. However, your spirit won't leave you alone—that is the nagging you feel in your soul. You have to tap into it with something other than your five natural senses. You have to make a leap of faith and simply ask God to baptize your soul so that you can live stronger, bolder, and more passionately for Him and in your calling or purpose.

You may think that once you're saved, this Holy Spirit firepower will automatically come over you. But consider this: the disciples certainly were saved—after all, they walked with Jesus and witnessed miracles and healings—yet they still doubted. They still lacked zeal and zest for Jesus. They denied Him. They betrayed Him. They fell asleep when their master asked them to pray with Him. A certain passion or fire (power) was missing. There is a difference between the Holy Spirit who comforts, convicts, and guides coming over your spirit on the day of your salvation and the baptism of the Holy Spirit coming over your soul and empowering you.

Let's try to understand this concept by picturing a person as a new home purchase. When you buy a house, you actually are buying two things: the actual structure and the land. Continuing with this analogy, let's imagine the house is your soul and the land or yard is your spirit. When you receive God's free gift of salvation by receiving Jesus Christ as your personal Lord and Savior, the Holy Spirit enters into your yard (your human spirit). However, God now wants to go one step further with you and come into your actual house (your soul), mainly because this is where you really live. You spend most of your time in the house as opposed to being outside in the front or back yard.

God wants you to be in full firepower mode so that you can operate at your fullest potential for His glory. Our souls require transformation to the Word and the Holy Spirit's moving to prevent conformation to the world. I like how Pastor Rod Parsley describes it: "The baptism of the spirit will do for you what a phone booth did for Clark Kent—it will change you into a different human being."[2]

Let me ask you a question: have you seen born-again Christians without the fire of the Holy Spirit in them? I don't know about you, but the sight sorely saddens my heart. They say they are not emotional people, but I bet if they were drowning in the deep ocean we would see a spark or two of emotion. They are passionate about their hobbies, their families, their jobs, their favorite sports teams, and so forth, but lack life in their souls because Jesus is not their Lord and His Spirit has not caught fire in their souls. The Bible says that he or she who has the Son has life! I'm convinced that timidity, fear, a lethargic spirit, excessive diplomacy, a powerless mind-set, or this eggshell-walking political correctness our society values steals life from our souls and should be replaced with a Holy Spirit fire that causes us to light up like a torch.

In the game of checkers, getting "kinged" increases our chances of winning. We are now able to jump over pieces, move backwards, and basically have the power to move freely around the board. You're "armed and dangerous!" When we are Holy Spirit "kinged" by the King of kings, our emotions are more stable, our mind-set becomes bolder, our peace is perfect, our joy is unspeakable, and we are free in our souls. Our marriage, job, confidence, boldness, wisdom, and life prosper. You live with more power! Your opponent (the devil) now has to pay closer attention to you.

Furthermore, when you have been "kinged" by the fire of the Holy Spirit, you understand that evangelism or witnessing is not optional but mandatory. It is now your calling, and the boldness that has been set in you will help you focus more on the calling than on your comfort zone. Evangelizing becomes a part of your life and not something you do to acquire brownie points or extra credit.

Let me ask you, what if God could use your "king me" status as a way to help change your community forever and bring more lost souls to Christ? What a difference maker you would be, right? You would be truly fulfilled in the knowledge and assurance that your existence has meaning. That's how it is. You notice the needs in others after you've been "kinged" because you have simply surrendered to the perfect works of Jesus Christ, the King of kings. You have acknowledged Him as Lord (in other words, your choices and opinions don't count anymore), and you live like you've been crowned with true power because the fire of the Holy Spirit now resides in you.

How Do We Become People of Power and Boldness "Kinged" by the Holy Spirit?

UNDERSTAND the Holy Spirit

Just because we are aware of something, this doesn't mean we know all there is to know about it. The Holy Spirit is the third person of the godly Trinity. He (not "it") gives us an appetite for transformation, a hunger and thirst for God and His presence.

EMBRACE the Holy Spirit

You embrace the Holy Spirit—or the Holy Ghost, as many call Him—with salvation (into your spirit), and you embrace Him with sanctification (into your soul), though it can certainly happen together with salvation. You don't get filled halfway; you get filled completely. We may try to understand the Holy Spirit, but we will never fully understand His work. Don't be too concerned with how much of the Spirit you have, but focus more on how much the Spirit has of you.

Everyone encounters the Spirit differently, but we should all strive to encounter Him. Do not fight off what you need to empower you to the next level of your spiritual maturity.

Many people do not fully embrace the Holy Spirit mainly because He has been misrepresented. We have been spooked by the concept of a spirit or ghost or because of some people's erratic and extreme behavior, perceived possession of some kind. However, just because you have unfortunately witnessed out-of-order scenarios in the house of God, it does not mean getting baptized in the Holy Ghost should be avoided or dismissed. Some people are just peculiar or dramatic. That does not mean, however, that being filled with the Spirit is wrong. If that were so, Jesus wouldn't have left Him for us. I don't know about you, but I don't want anything God doesn't want to give me. By the same token, I desperately want everything that God does want to give me, knowing that it will enhance or empower my discipleship status.

The Holy Spirit leads us into the knowledge of who Jesus is, and when we move into the fullness of this knowledge and begin to operate in faith, we are then baptized with the Holy Spirit or Ghost. The Holy Ghost is the power of the glorified body of Jesus Christ, the power of the Son Himself manifested in us.

EMPLOY THE HOLY SPIRIT

In a nutshell, fire yourself and hire the Spirit. Let Him work *on* you, not just *for* you. In our ministry, we've embraced a made-up mind-set that we will conduct fervent prayers, operate in love and compassion as Jesus commanded, and allow the Holy Spirit to roam free! We are simply embedding sound and powerful roots that will help us stay focused on our calling, mission, and vision despite the circumstances in our lives. When roots run deep, you need not tremble at the howl of the wind. I hope I am conveying this message in a way that will help you embrace this powerful Helper, because:

- If you're going to speak the truth in love, you'll need His powerful help.

- If you're going to love your enemies, you'll need His powerful help.

- If you're going to live with boldness, you'll need His powerful help.

- If you're going to witness and not stay silent, you'll need His powerful help.

- If you're going to do the things Jesus did, you'll need His powerful help.

- If you're going to live as more than a conqueror, you'll need His powerful help.

- If you're going to have self-control over your body and words, you'll need His powerful help.

- If you're going to live with more grace and faith, you'll need His powerful help.

- If you need the courage to witness, stand
  firm without compromise in your walk, and
  invite people to church, you'll need His
  powerful help.

This Helper, Comforter, and Counselor is necessary
not only for these things but also for many other things
that God will eventually disclose to you so that you may
embark as His chosen instrument for His ultimate glory.

Having the fire of the Holy Spirit baptize your soul is the
extra power we need to walk in His perfect will, fulfilling
our calling and purpose and all He wants us to do for
His Kingdom glory. Imagine a boat stuck on a sandbar,
totally immobilized. Holy Spirit fire is the tide that rises
and releases the boat so that it can get free to return to
deeper waters. Once you open yourself to being filled
with the Spirit of God, life changes, because you possess
a supernatural connection that will help you maximize
your earthly potential, not to mention fulfill His purpose
in your life with unflinching boldness.

WHY DO WE NEED THE FIRE
OF THE HOLY SPIRIT?

IT EMPOWERS US WITH BOLDNESS, COURAGE, AND
OBEDIENCE TO PREACH THE GOSPEL

> And He said to them, "Go into all the world and
> preach the gospel to every creature."
>
> —MARK 16:15

Prayer is not enough to help people go from darkness
to the light. The gospel is news, and news is only pertinent
when it's shared with others.

It allows us to be in UNITY for the purposes and plans God has for us

> When the Day of Pentecost had fully come, they were all with one accord [unity] in one place. And suddenly there came a sound from heaven, as of a rushing mighty wind, and it filled the whole house where they were sitting.
>
> —Acts 2:1–2

We are purpose-driven people, but we also need to be Holy Spirit–driven people. No man or woman can give you their anointing, for your anointing is from God and it is unique. This fire of the Holy Spirit gives you promotion and vindication. You don't have to overly promote yourself; you just have to go through the fire.

It HELPS us in our time of need, trouble, and crisis .

> And I will pray the Father, and He will give you another Helper, that He may abide with you forever.
>
> —John 14:16

Four things are needed in order for the Holy Spirit fire to catch on:

1. BELIEF that it has happened before, as recorded in the Bible, and it's still happening today;

2. Salvation, or to be WASHED in the blood. Spiritual conversion mixed with childlike faith is irresistible to God. Don't just get enough of Jesus to stay out of hell; get

enough to make Him Lord, and you can live a more powerful life;

3. UNITY with the body of Christ, meaning your fellow brothers and sisters in Christ; and

4. UTTERANCE—it must be spoken (which is an evident but necessary sign). "And they were all filled with the Holy Ghost, and began to speak with other tongues, as the Spirit gave them utterance" (Acts 2:4, KJV).

Nothing happens unless it's spoken! Many want God to perform miracles but don't even voice a word of prayer or proclamation. Faith is praying in a language we don't understand, to a God we haven't seen, to acquire wisdom we can't imagine. We serve an omnipotent God, not an impotent God. He is a consuming fire of passion. Feel secure knowing that the Holy Spirit will give you words, but keep in mind that He is not going to pray for you. You will be emitting the words with your own voice, using your own tongue and mouth. The Holy Spirit will gift you with a prayer language of your own, but you will be doing the talking.

Let me interject something important here. I know many people have abused this gift in churches over the years. They desire to appear "holier than thou" with their extreme articulations and actions and out-of-godly-order. However, just because the gift of tongues has been abused, this does not mean it should be dismissed. You owe it to yourself to be baptized in the Spirit.

Speaking in tongues edifies the church, but praying in tongues edifies you. It is like charging the battery of the human spirit. The Holy Spirit will bring the prompting, desire, or urge to speak. It's an utterance that your mind won't understand because it is coming from your spirit man. At first it may be only a few syllables, but the more you pray, the more your language will grow. Just be natural, real, and relaxed. Understand that if you take one step toward Jesus, He will take many more steps toward you. The times are urgent, God is on the move, and now is the moment to ask God to ignite His Holy Spirit fire in your soul!

INFILLING PRAYER

If you are yearning for Holy Spirit boldness and power, I urge you to pray this prayer:

> *Heavenly Father, I come to You in the name of Jesus to thank You because I am Your child. By faith I now receive the gift of the Holy Spirit with the evidence of speaking in other tongues as the Holy Spirit gives me utterance. I release my fears and my pride to You. I relax my mind, I trust in Your Word, and I shift my mind to Spirit prayer utterance, in the name of Jesus!*

Once you are engaged in a heavenly language, just speak whatever comes naturally out of your mouth without worrying about engaging your mind. It's your spirit speaking to God, who Himself is a Spirit. Trust God for guidance and trust that your words are gradually filling your soul. Trust the process God has created for your empowerment!

I don't know what you may be going through right now; perhaps you're caught up in a major fire of your own that is causing the walls of life to get progressively hotter like the furnace did for the Hebrew boys. But I know for certain that when you engage your faith in

God's Holy Spirit fire, you can get through it! God can be trusted, but make sure you are ALL IN for Him!

NOTES

PREFACE

1.   BrainyQuote, "Jim Rohn Quotes," accessed July 19, 2017, https://www.brainyquote.com/quotes/quotes/j/jimrohn385514.html.

CHAPTER 1: GOD'S WILL OR YOUR WILL?

1.   Heriberto Alonso, *Blessed, Balanced & Complete: Flesh vs. Spirit Living* (Miami: Xulon, 2008), 116–117.

2.   AZ Quotes, "John C. Maxwell Quotes," accessed July 19, 2017, www.azquotes.com/quote/359431.

CHAPTER 2: THE POWER OF CHOICES AND DECISIONS

1.   As quoted in Myles Monroe, *Understanding the Purpose and Power of Prayer* (New Kensington, PA: Whitaker House, 2002).

CHAPTER 3: WALKING IN THE FEAR OF THE LORD

1.   Goodreads, "Billy Graham," accessed July 19, 2017, http://www.goodreads.com/quotes/833766-it-is-the-holy-spirit-s-job-to-convict-god-s-job.

CHAPTER 5: FORGET THE PAST AND EMBRACE THE NEW

1.   This chapter was inspired by the counseling teachings of one of my past mentors, Apostle Lee Harris.

CHAPTER 7: COMMITTED TO LOVING RIGHT

1.   This chapter was inspired by a marriage sermon from one of my mentors, Apostle Duane Swilley.

CHAPTER 9: DEFEATING DOUBLE-MINDEDNESS

1.   This chapter was inspired by a sermon from Apostle Ron Carpenter of Redemption Church.

Chapter 10: Moving Past Stuck

1.   Goodreads, "William Booth Quotes," accessed July 19, 2017, https://www.goodreads.com/author/quotes/151267.William_Booth.

Chapter 11: Are You a Fan or a Follower?

1.   Justin D. Lyons, "Hernán Cortés: Master of the Conquest," HistoryNet, December 28, 2016, accessed July 26, 2017, http://www.historynet.com/hernan-cortes-master-of-the-conquest.htm.

Chapter 15: Tenaciously Trusting God Wholeheartedly

1.   This chapter was inspired by the "Kingdom Faith" sermon from Apostle Rufus Troup of Solid Rock Church.

Chapter 16: Embracing the Fire of the Holy Spirit

1.   Inspired by a sermon from Evangelist Reinhard Bonnke of Christ for all Nations.
2.   As quoted in Dick Bernal, *Shaking Hands with God* (Bloomington, MN: Chosen Books, 2008).

ABOUT THE AUTHOR

HERIBERTO "HERY" ALONSO is a licensed and ordained minister, author, evangelist, inspirational speaker, and life-coach (health-mind-relationships). He is a graduate of Alpha & Omega Bible Institute and earned a bachelor's degree in business administration from Florida International University.

Hery's parents were very instrumental in bringing him into the ways of the Lord. When he was nine years old, he accepted Jesus Christ as his Lord and Savior and was baptized seven years later. Beginning in his early twenties, Hery went through a twelve–year period of backsliding and spiritual disconnect. He says it was this separation from God that caused him a lot of unnecessary turmoil and lack of peace. After repenting, he rededicated his life to Christ and returned to the ways of the Lord at the age of thirty-four. However, he admits that he still wasn't totally surrendered, which caused him to continue to experience much frustration and failure until years later, when he finally decided to be completely ALL IN.

In 2004, Hery began conducting and teaching Bible studies from the living room of his home. Today, his teachings have elevated to what is now **RiseUp Outreach Center**, a church in Miami, Florida. Services are held on Thursday evenings and also are broadcasted live to a national and international audience with hundreds of viewers. He teaches his listeners, viewers, and readers to focus on two particular scriptures: 2 Thessalonians 3:13—"Don't ever get tired of doing what is right" and 1 Peter 5:8—"Be well balanced, be vigilant and cautious at all times" (AMPC).

His first book, titled *Blessed, Balanced & Complete,* is based on his own life experiences as well as Bible teachings, and is available in Spanish and English. As a minister, he speaks at various churches and institutions on topics such as Kingdom Principles; Health and Fitness; Relationships; Motivation for Success; Healing the Soul from Past Experiences; and Prioritization and Balance of Life.

Hery says that ever since God called him into full-time ministry, he has wholeheartedly embraced his purpose. He currently resides in Miami with his wife, Sandra, and their three children.

ALSO BY HERIBERTO "HERY" ALONSO

BLESSED, BALANCED & COMPLETE (ENGLISH)

How to live a balanced life in body, mind, and spirit so you can live with more inner freedom, fulfillment, and less stress.

BENDECIDO, EQUILIBRADO Y COMPLETO (SPANISH)

Cómo vivir una vida equilibrada en su cuerpo, mente y espíritu para que pueda vivir con más libertad interior, satisfacción y menos estrés.

ALSO BY HERIBERTO "HERY" ALONSO

BLESSED, BALANCED & COMPLETE (ENGLISH)

How to live a balanced life in body, mind, and spirit so you can live with more inner freedom, fulfillment, and less stress.

BENDECIDO, EQUILIBRADO Y COMPLETO (SPANISH)

Cómo vivir una vida equilibrada en su cuerpo, mente y espíritu para que pueda vivir con más libertad interior, satisfacción y menos estrés.

CONTACT THE AUTHOR

To contact Pastor Alonso, please write to:

Alonso Inspirational Ministries

P.O. Box 832407

Miami, FL 33283-2407

Email: hery@alonsoministries.org

Website: www.AlonsoMinistries.org